Architecture of the World

Pierre Charpentrat
Henri Stierlin (Ed.)

Baroque
Italy and Central Europe

Photos: Peter Heman
Preface: Hans Scharoun

Benedikt Taschen

Editor of Series	Henri Stierlin
Plans	Georges Berthoud EPF SIA
English Translation	Carol Brown

Contents

''Ni le Classique ni le Baroque n'ont d'existence en soi, comme des réalités existant indépendamment des hommes et des œuvres. On ne les accepte pas, on ne les choisit pas comme on choisit un vêtement ou un cheval... On ne définit pas un style, une civilisation, comme des valeurs extérieures aux hommes qui les utilisent sans y rien changer...''

Pierre Francastel

Preface

By Hans Scharoun

The Message of Baroque

The climate of Baroque, the various elements which characterized the buildings, and the origins and styles of the architects of the period are all dealt with exhaustively in this book. Thus, demands of the present have been amply fulfilled by illustrating our connections with that time. The following observations may serve to underline the necessity for a critical comparison correlating current trends with historical phenomena.

If we do not subscribe to Spengler's view that all great civilizations are so many defeats, but follow Hugo Häring, who defends the genesis of mankind – its integration with the actual creative process – we see the great civilizations as the tasks which are given to mankind to be dealt with step by step in the workrooms, in the field of tension of rational and irrational, the rational which had its roots in the Greek sphere of influence. From now on it was linked with geometrical forms such as the rectangle (Greece) and the circle (Rome) until it attained the two-poled ellipse which gave the Baroque, especially in its Late German form, character and tension. This finds expression particularly in Baroque church architecture. Its character is a result not only of liberation from dogmatic petrification, which was the final fate of the Renaissance; nor is it an emotional illustration of the Reformed Religion. The ecstatic quality of Baroque art in its radical purposefulness accords with the pattern of behavior of Baroque man in general. Civilization is a living homogeneous structure.

In this connection let us focus on problems of structure that have again assumed importance in contemporary architecture. In the Middle Ages, planning and building were subordinated to the requirements of religious symbolism; the Baroque approach relates man directly to interior space. In Southern Germany, especially, it replaces the traditional spatial conception by open space. This, though on another plane, is also a present-day claim. In 'Handbuch der Kulturgeschichte,' Willi Fleming mentions the contradictions characteristic of Baroque man: his extrovert self-centredness and his fervor for the hereafter. From this sprang conflicts and mannerisms in architecture and behavior in order to 'adapt the world completely to the glorification of the ego.' The oscillations of parabola and ellipse signify passionate involvement of the individual with the fathomless universe. The monastery library at Metten demonstrates this conflict between the craving for individual importance and human endeavor: in a symbolic manner it represents a dramatic yet obviously uncomfortable state of mind, knowledge and power held in balance.

The new Philharmonic building, Berlin, by Hans Scharoun

The main hall, Philharmonic building, Berlin

Another problem of contemporary architecture is the attention given to the 'action.' The Baroque, too, saw structures adapted to proceedings which found their expression in various types of church plan. This also applies to the arrangement of theater design – as, for example, in Bayreuth. The rigid seating plan of this building reflects the social structure of the time. The stalls were reserved for the populace and could become the scene of the action when, for instance, they performed country dances. This purposeful direction of consciousness towards an object is a matter of intentional imagination. What concerns, stimulates and excites us today, is the manifold, ecstatic and, in its successful moments, timeless result achieved. A radical opinion here becomes a work of art. The creation of a second natural world, worked on since by later epochs, found in the Baroque its first spontaneous realization as impulsive invasion of nature and reality – thus the great layouts of parks endeavoring to recreate nature, and the delight in robot-like automats.

What happens, takes place in an atmosphere of power-politics. But one thing is remarkable – while secular building remains largely a question of exteriors (apart from a few staterooms and a lavish display of staircases), the churches achieve a unity of component parts, whether their mood is tragic, gay or dramatic. Here is another association with today – the stirring of the creative imagination in science and art, especially in architecture, tends towards a restoration of unity.

Once more we must stress that the richness of earthly power is expressed in structural geometrical forms. The Baroque repeats these forms, and arches them over with the two-poled ellipse, the discovery of this last great stylistic period. This century-old individualistic civilization is replaced by a subjective 'Weltanschanning' and ends in authoritarian absolution.

Nowadays, artistic development is no longer left to individual intuition, as with the Baroque. Humanity has a new task. Yet we could never perceive it in its entirety without knowledge of what has preceded it. It is therefore extremely important that we should concern ourselves with the work of the Baroque which still influences our world today.

Berlin 1964

Concert hall of the Philharmonic building, showing the irregular galleries surrounding the orchestra

Introduction

To give architecture its rightful place in the Baroque world is more difficult than would at first appear. Writers today, fired with enthusiasm for Baroque as such, tend to see its churches and palaces merely as the triumphant flowering of a perfectly uniform type of civilization. In some parts of Europe and America, the seventeenth, and part of the eighteenth centuries constitute a clearly defined period having as essential qualities an inextricable complexity and an indivisible plenitude.

It would be no contradiction to suppose that a Roman church, an abbey by the Danube, one of Bernini's statues or Pietro da Cortona's frescoes are brought to life by the same twisted forms, the same tensions, and the same brilliant interplay of light and shadow. Heinrich Wölfflin was the most famous of those who argued along these lines, striving to define criteria common to the three arts of architecture, painting and sculpture and uniting them throughout the Baroque world. If we consider this century and a half of intense productivity and thought, in which the violent eddies of the Renaissance and the Reformation were developed and merged into modern thought and visual processes as a single entity, it is tempting to widen our range of associations and analogies still further.

For some years now, many historians and critics, particularly in Germany, have been using the term 'Baroque Music.' Indeed, the generation that included Corelli, Vivaldi and Scarlatti, born in 1653, 1678 and 1685 respectively, was contemporary with the height of the Baroque period in Italy. In 1700, J. S. Bach and Handel were both fifteen, the same age as the architects (including Balthazar Neumann, the most original of them all) who were to give eighteenth century Germany its external appearance. The parallel does not end with the time factor: in this case, the influence of Vivaldi assumed a rôle comparable to that played

The Scala Regia, Vatican, by Bernini (after a contemporary engraving)

so often by the influence of the masters of the Seicento in the development of German Baroque architecture.

Recently, French writers have been trying to ressuscitate a literary background to the three arts united by the analyses of Wölfflin. They have brought to light a lyricism which is explained and justified by its closeness to Bernini; at the same time it strips his work of all superfluousness and helps us to recognize the obsessions of an entire society, where the nineteenth century could only distinguish a series of individual whims. The Germans have rediscovered their Baroque writers, including the poets Gryphius and Hofmannswaldau, and the novelist Grimmelshausen, all of whom were born at the time of the Defenestration of Prague and grew up amid the horrors of the Thirty Years' War. Angelus Silesius was another of these writers: born a Lutheran, he died a Roman Catholic priest, thus becoming one of the symbols of Rome's reconquest, usually associated with the rise of the new architecture.

The period of the mystic Silesius also lent individual color to learning. Following the example of Giedion, we will have to examine the problem of the relationship between the conception of space, constructional techniques and the mathematics of the Baroque which abolished certain concepts, bringing tangible shell of matter into disrepute and balancing it between two stretches of infinity.

Microscopes and telescopes, the chief aids to this enquiry, machines for the extension of the world's frontiers, were transformed into bibelots. Their feet were carved with Rococo shells, curved and notched like angels' wings, and they were displayed with chinoiserie and Meissen porcelain, and fans in elegant inlaid cabinets. The setting of life had been imprisoned, and conquered in its entirety. The number of recent Baroque exhibitions, presenting fragments of works of art next to everyday objects, have made a powerful contribution to our recognition of this unity, turning the abundance which accompanies the architecture into an individual circumstance, the expression of a trend that simultaneously produced coaches, poops for sailing galleys, ball dresses and toilet articles. In the case of furniture, the relationship is perceptible to the point of becoming equivocal.

Seventeenth-century cabinet-makers clearly attempted to give a monumental appearance to other creations. Within them they arranged yet more colonnades, opening up perspectives similar to those of theatrical scenery or the naves of churches. To us they give the impression of rows of gigantic cupboards, just as the indented gables of the Grand'-Place at Brussels did to Baudelaire. The sofas and console tables of the Venetian Brustolon, with cherubs' heads emerging from tight scrolls, suggest the rhythmic themes scattered by religious artists throughout the vast interiors of their churches, lending

them a strange, haunting power. Other Italian luxury products – lace, embroidery, Venetian chandeliers – were distributed still more widely, giving Europe a taste for arabesques and glittering reflection, fickle combinations of brilliance and emptiness, subtle shapes outlined and disguised in ephemeral materials.

From this cohesion there finally arose a strongly individual Baroque man. Historians have endeavored with a greater or lesser degree of objectivity (sometimes praiseworthy but more often condemnatory), to reconstruct this

Design for ceiling decoration; eighteenth-century Italian school. Color-wash, Fatio Collection

Design for eighteenth-century ceiling. Library of Art and Archeology, Geneva (Fatio Collection)

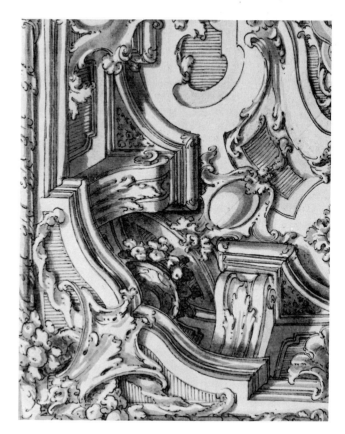

Italian Baroque ornamentation, showing trophies, garlands, cherubs flowering over the architectural structure (after an unpublished drawing; Fatio Collection)

being who so stubbornly tried to reform and distort the world.

We must be careful not to exaggerate the importance of this teeming background: on closer examination, each branch of art compels us to grant it a wide range of independence.

The example of Germany, home of the pan-Baroque, is an eloquent invitation to caution. The parallel between Bach and Neumann is scarcely more significant than any other parallel: both men, together with their arts, developed in two different worlds and did not meet at any point. Bach's cantatas were composed in a city that was one of the most austere strongholds of anti-Baroque Germany. As for the so-called Baroque poets, the architectural background into which they attempted to blend, was first and foremost one of the Middle Ages and Renaissance. Not until the time of their deaths, between 1660-1680, did German architecture begin the search for a new style. Many of the characteristics of the 'Baroque man' who stirred up and endured the horrors of the Thirty Years' War were still those of a sixteenth-century man; his principal contribution to the development of German Baroque consisted in clearing building sites for his descendants by dint of pillaging and burning the buildings of former ages.

Nor can the various branches of art at Rome be unreservedly compared. They were far from achieving a unanimity established round great Baroque artists like Bernini and Borromini.

A strong classical or classicizing current can be felt through the sculpture and particularly the painting of the Seicento. Guido Reni, Domenico Chino and Guercino, favorites of the arch-critic of the Baroque, Stendhal, did not die until 1666, a year before Borromini. The generation following these Bolognese artists included Andrea

Design for decoration, by Fernando Bibiena

Sacchi, the contemporary and rival of Pietro da Cortona, and the sculptors, Algardi and Ruquesnoy – a generation of near geniuses with whom Poussin could associate without seeming either a revolutionary or a reactionary. Indeed, Algardi's reputation was such as to influence Bernini for several years, causing him to moderate some of his works. Twenty-five years later, the conciliatory eclectic, Maratta (1625-1713), opposed himself to the Baroque Gaulli, symbolizing the strength of the resistance and showing that the age of Mengs was not far distant.

In each of these successive rivalries, the champions of Baroque painting were essentially fresco painters whose activities were directly linked to architecture; the supporters of classicism were those for who painting constituted an independent art. Here, in particular, architecture harmonized with the subordinate art which completed and supplemented it. As we shall see later, the great compositions of Pietro da Cortona, Pozzo and Gaulli transfigured churches built before the Baroque period, then out of fashion, but too new for reconstruction. The connection is, after all, one of subordination rather than analogy. In countries where the architecture is Baroque, unity is in proportion to its tyrannical vitality. While there are no more parallels or meeting-points, more exclusive attention is paid to the art identified with the age, which tends to reduce the others to the level of minor arts. During these first two thirds of the eighteenth century, in Austria and Bohemia, Wurtemberg and Bavaria, scarcely any lack of harmony is discernible. A common frenzy of building seized princes, bishops and monks; painters were merely given the right to decorate ceilings, sculptors to embellish staircases, crossroads and parks. The coherence of the Baroque world, in so far as it is not mere illusion, is more a matter of function than of aesthetics; it is not made up of jets that simultaneously form one level cascade: it is the result of a conscious organization and gradation of society.

The architects modified the significance of these painted and sculptured forms in order to gain their assistance. We shall try to show how these same forms contribute to the construction of an architectural space. Exhibitions, however necessary and exciting they may be, distort our vision in this respect. A section of an altarpiece may resemble the piece of furniture next to it, but this resemblance is due more than anything else to both objects being displayed in close proximity. In church, the altarpiece belongs to a different world. One of Brustolon's cherubs smiles or grimaces as an individual. In church the cherubs are hemmed in by garlands and clusters of flowers, or are hidden behind symbolic objects: out of a fairly realistic motif, the architect and his assistant have created a supporting cadence, an element of syntax. Architecture is not an individual phenomenon, but plays the part of a framework, governing the plan.

Italian eighteenth-century painting gives us final proof of its power. It is not a question of knowing whether one can call this style of painting Baroque, but merely of freeing it from the astonishing predominance of architectural themes. It springs from the nostalgia of generations deprived of great builders, who were unconsciously preparing the way for the age of the archaeologists and pasticheurs. This drying up of the creative life-force can be partly accounted for by the thorough exactitude and precision of artists such as Pannini, Canaletto and Bellotto. There is more to it than this, however. Wölfflin declared that Baroque architecture gravitated towards sculpture, and sculpture towards painting. Conversely, architecture, with the help of the free, everchanging substitute of stage scenery, ended by building pictorial fantasies and directing the most poetic forms of fancy. For the Bolognese architect Bigari, it was no longer a question of reproducing real monuments

Study for a Baroque interior (after an unpublished
eighteenth-century Italian drawing; Fatio Collection)

but of giving his dreams monumental forms. By
now, architecture had so monopolized and re-
defined space, that every study of this element
was couched in architectural terms. Height was
measured in terms of columns and storeys,
depth in terms of the curve of a balcony, and
perspective became synonymous with the slant
of a gallery. It was Piranesi, however, who paid
most willing tribute to the sovereign art of the
Baroque age with his wild fantasies of walls and
roof beams. But his super-human creations

respect the laws of construction; the haunting
quality of these visions springs from their
technical verisimilitude. Nevertheless, revolt is
near, and the reign of the architect is drawing
to its close. The infinite confusion of Piranesi's
towers and bridges fills space with its incontro-
vertible patterns, but, simultaneously, this
artist heralds the century of ruins, the age in
which men were enthusiastic about fallen buildings, edifices overgrown with vegetation.

Baroque architecture covers a vast amount of territory, of which only part is dealt with in this book. There is no discussion of Spain, Portugal or Latin America, which together make up half the Baroque world, no less fascinating than the other; another volume in this series will be devoted to them. Of the Slavonic countries only Bohemia and Moravia are included: the subject of Russian Baroque, and the 'Narychkin Baroque' in particular, would have necessitated lengthy digressions to explain their individual historical background. What is, perhaps, more regrettable is the omission of Poland. Polish religious architecture of the seventeenth and eighteenth centuries, despite its delightful originality, especially in its early period, is related to Italo-German Baroque. Nevertheless, it seemed better not to discuss it at all rather than give it insufficient space.

It may be argued that secular architecture has been subordinated to that of religious buildings. Is this a reaction against the view that still too often disputes the religious character of the Baroque? Or is it an assimilation of the Baroque with the Counter-Reformation? In actual fact, the Church, after the Council of Trent, should have produced the opposite of Baroque – and almost did. There is, however, no doubt that only religious themes inspired strikingly original investigations in Italy and Central Europe. In the secular world, decisive changes took place elsewhere; the most 'modern' château of this period, which witnessed the construction of so many, was clearly Versailles. To a certain extent, the Baroque meant a break with tradition, creative genius and discovery, and did not take kindly to juxtapositions and divisions, tending to unify space; it adapted itself badly to a type of building where, despite a supreme disregard for so-called comfort, domestic functions of various kinds imposed a radical disproportionate partitioning of space. As has so often been said, the Baroque seemed a tireless quest – it

was difficult to produce totally new reinventions – even vaster buildings in the midst of whose bulk the architect had occasionally to leave, like saving straws, a mere whisper, or silence. So it finally came about that these buildings were less Baroque châteaux than Baroque façades, staterooms and staircases. The churches are exceptional in that the solitary voice of the architect is continually heard. This is the first of the analogies between the Baroque and Gothic ages that must be stressed.

The need to bring this book into line with the rest of the series has excluded a purely chronological approach and led to the adoption of four successive viewpoints. The first chapter is historical and offers a schematic outline of the spread of Baroque architecture from Rome, from the start of Bernini's career to the victory of Neo-Classicism, and briefly places the chief artists of the movement against their background. The next two chapters deal with religious architecture. The first discusses the 'shells' of the churches: their elevations, façades and particularly, their plans. The latter caused so much trouble, objects as they were of many thoughts and second thoughts, that they ended up as works of art themselves. Designed and contrived with intense care, critically examined by the architect in charge and subsequently remodeled to suit his wishes, the plans are often contradicted, or at least partly concealed, by the development of the interior space. The third chapter outlines this purely Baroque phenomenon, and, in addition, describes the part played by what is incorrectly termed decoration. It also includes a certain amount of technical information. Finally, the fourth chapter discusses several basic features of secular architecture and attempts to place the monuments of the Baroque against their town or country backgrounds and to define their connections with exterior space.

Plates

Rome

21 **S Agnese in the Piazza Navone.** The wide façade, about 150 feet in length, bordering the west side of the Piazza. The width of the nave, where it touches the façade, corresponds to that of the center portico. The total width of the transept exactly equals that of the steps leading to the entrance. In the right foreground, Bernini's Fountain of the Rivers (1648-1651).

22 The choir seen from the entrance to the left transept. A bas-relief by Ercole Ferrata, the **Stoning of St Emerentia** (1660) occupies a niche between the choir and the right transept.

23 The drum of the dome, two of the pendentives, and the entablature. Three barrel vaults separate the pendentives: on the left the one belonging to the choir, in the center the one belonging to the right transept and that on the right to the narthex. They form a perfect Greek Cross.

24 One of Bernini's Rivers, the dome and the right-hand tower.

25 **S Ivo-della-Sapienza.** The exterior of Borromini's dome, dominating Giacomo della Porta's 'cortile' (1575). A false drum concealing the lower part of the actual dome. The lantern with its concave facets is surmounted by a spiral.

26 An unaccented feature of the nave; a bay with a convex back wall between the choir and one of the small apses framing the entrance.

27 Interior of the dome. The line of the cornice emphasizes the ternary rhythm, especially the three accented features, the concave recesses corresponding to the choir and the two small apses opposite.

28 The back of the concave recesses.

29 **S Andrea-del-Quirinale.** The entrance to the choir from the right hand side of the nave. Red columns with white capitals.

30 The dome seen from the entrance. The angels and the 'putti' (cherubs) above the windows and the winged heads below the lantern are white. The coffers of the dome are gilded.

31 Angels and cherubs in the choir.

32 The 'Glory' in the choir. Below, the 'Crucifixion of St Andrew,' the picture surmounting the high altar. Above, a small dome, the base of which forms the center of the 'Glory;' from it the top lighting characteristic of Bernini, descends into the small space of the choir. This small dome is invisible from most of the nave.

33 **S Maria-in-Portico.** Note the thickness of the façade and the varied arrangement of the coupled columns.

34 The choir from the narrow section of the nave, looking across the space lit by the dome. The widest portion of the nave, in the form of a Greek Cross, is behind the photograph.

35 The columns of the narrow section of the nave, and, beyond, those at the base of the dome.

36 'A multitude of fluted shafts.'

Genoa

37 **The University.** First-floor gallery and second-floor staircase.

38 General view, from the entrance to the courtyard.

39 The vestibule.

40 The courtyard from the first-floor staircase.

Turin

41 **S Lorenzo.** The dome from the courtyard of the Palazzo.

42 Ground-level of the nave, showing three sides of the octagon. In the center, the choir, lit by a secondary dome whose base is visible. Dominant color: old rose. Volutes and statues are white. Occasional touches of green, yellow and black.

44 Interior of the dome, showing the eight ribs reminiscent of Moslem and Spanish Romanesque architecture. The height of the ribs corresponds to that of the drum.

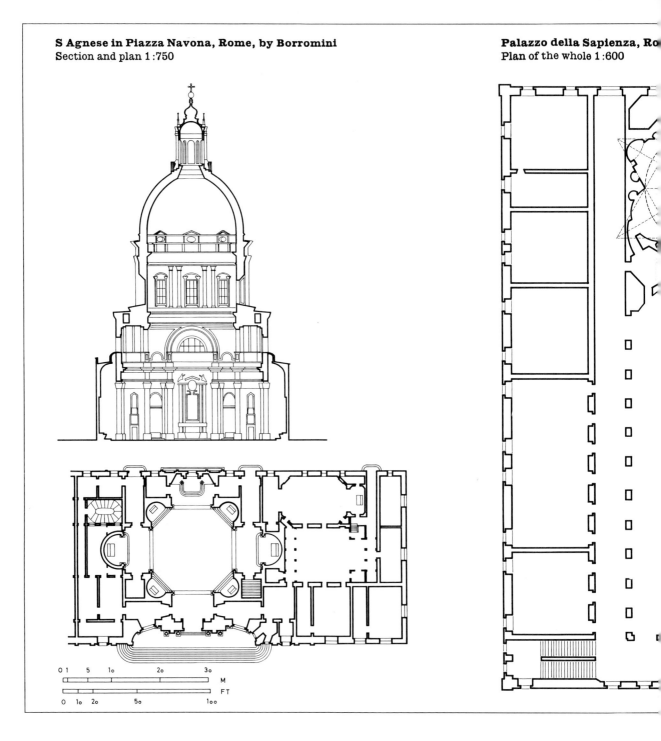

S Agnese in Piazza Navona, Rome, by Borromini
Section and plan 1:750

Palazzo della Sapienza, Ro
Plan of the whole 1:600

O 1 5   1o   2o   3o
                                    M
                                    FT
O   1o 2o   5o   1oo

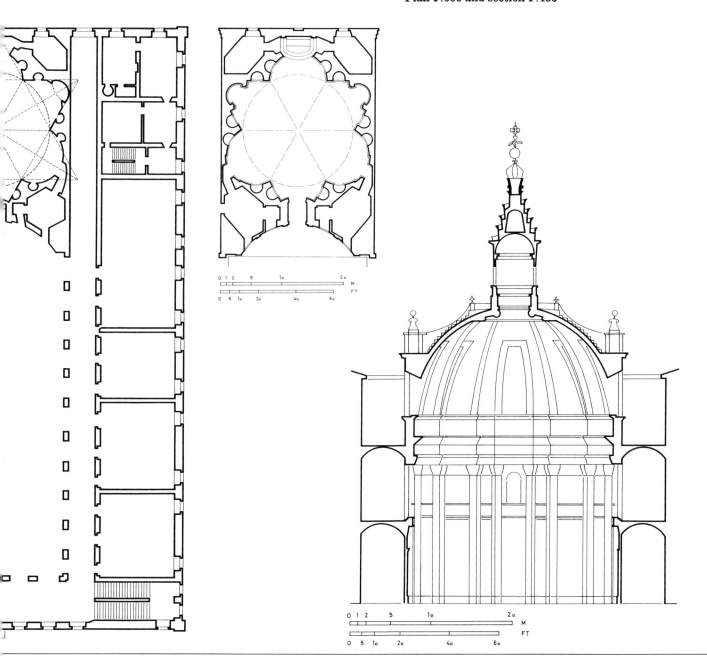

0 1 2   5   1o   2o   M
                                                      FT
0 5 1o   2o   4o   6o

0 1 2   5   1o   2o   M
                                                      FT
0 5 1o   2o   4o   6o

Notes

Rome

S Agnese in Piazza Navona

Begun August 15, 1652, by Carlo Rainaldi in collaboration with his father, Girolamo, for Innocent X and the Pamphili family. The following year, Francesco Borromini replaced the Rainaldi: he modified the plan and designed the façade. Later he fell out with his works leader and Carlo Rainaldi resumed control of the work in 1657; he simplified the upper section of the façade and added to the heavy interior decoration. The tower was not finished until 1666. The stucco work was done by Ercole Ferrata and Antonio Raggi. The frescoes, rare in churches built by the great architects of this generation, are by G. B. Gaulli (pendentives) and Ciro Ferri (dome).

S Ivo-della-Sapienza

Church of the Roman Archiginnasio, which later became the University of Rome. Begun by Borromini in 1642; most of the structure completed in 1650. Decoration finished in 1660 while Borromini was carrying out various tasks in the Renaissance buildings of the Sapienza. Borromini was born in 1599 at Bissone on the Lake of Lugano. He was an apprentice sculptor in Milan, then a stone-carver in Rome about 1615. In St Peter's and later in the Palazzo Barberini, he worked as assistant to Maderno and later, Bernini. Broke with the latter in 1632. Two years later, he built the nave and cloister of S Carlo-alle-Quattro-Fontane, after which he worked on the Palazzo Spada and the Palazzo Falconieri, and built the Oratory of S Filippo Neri. In 1646, after S Ivo, he undertook the reconstruction of the nave of S Giovanni-in-Laterano, and, in 1653, the same year as S Agnese, he began erecting the drum of the dome and the campanile of S Andrea-delle-Fratte. After 1662, built the façade of S Carlo-alle-Quattro-Fontane and the church and façade of the Collegio di Propaganda Fide. Borromini died in 1667.

S Andrea-del-Quirinale

Commissioned from Bernini by Cardinal Camillo Pamphili for the novices of the Jesuit Order. Begun in 1658. Decoration completed about 1670. The stuccos are by Antonio Raggi, a pupil of Bernini. Gian Lorenzo Bernini was born in Naples in 1598 and was, first, sculptor to Cardinal Scipione Borghese. In 1624 he erected the Baldacchino for St Peter's and in 1629 succeeded Maderno as architect of the Basilica. In 1637, he decided to add towers to the façade, but the southern one was demolished in 1646. In 1639, he was commissioned to do the tomb of Urban VIII; in 1645, the Cornaro chapel; 1650, Palazzo Ludovisi; 1657, the colonnade of St Peter's. About 1660, he built his three churches: S Tomaso at Castel-Gandolfo, S Andrea-del-Quirinale, and S Maria-dell'-Assunzione at Ariccia. 1664, the Palazzo Chigi. He went to Paris in 1665 to design for the Louvre; he died in 1680.

S Maria-in-Campitelli (also known as S Maria-in-Portico) by Carlo Rainaldi

Votive church commemorating the end of the plague of 1656. It houses a miraculous image of the Virgin formerly worshipped in a smaller church on the same site. Building lasted from 1663 to 1667. Carlo Rainaldi (1611-1691) built the façade of S Andrea-della-Valle in 1661 and in 1662 began the small twin churches in the Piazza del Popolo.

Genoa

University

By Bartolomeo (before 1590-1657). The first plans were submitted to the Jesuits in 1630. Work began in 1634 and lasted twelve years.

Turin

S Lorenzo

Begun by Guarini in 1668. Mostly built by 1679, but not completed until 1687. Guarino Guarini (1624-1683) was born at Modena. He entered the Theatine Order and left for Rome in 1639. Then Professor of Philosophy in Modena, appointed head of his college in 1655, against the wishes of the Duke, who banished him; he was in exile for 25 years. In 1660, he was professor at Messina where he designed various churches, including that of the Padri Somaschi and designed the façade of the Annunziata. Transferred to Paris in 1662, where he designed Sainte-Anne-La-Royale, which was completed, in a considerably altered version, by 1720 and demolished in 1823. In 1666, he settled in Turin, and Carlo Emmanuele II of Savoy commissioned him to complete the Cappella della SS Sindone. After S Lorenzo, he built the church of S Filippo Neri, the Palazzo Carignano and the Collegio dei Nobili.

28

33

42

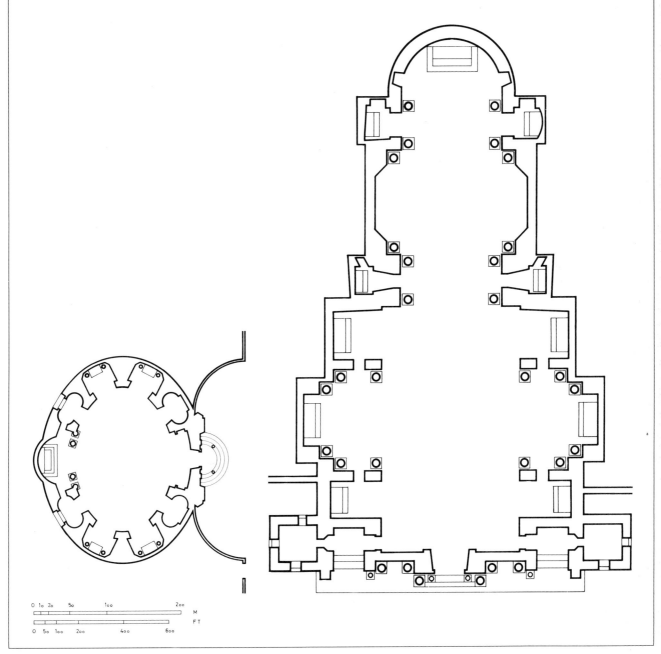

0 1o 2o   5o   1oo   2oo   M
                                                          F T
0   5o 1oo   2oo   4oo   6oo

45

The University, Genoa, by Bianco
Plan 1:500

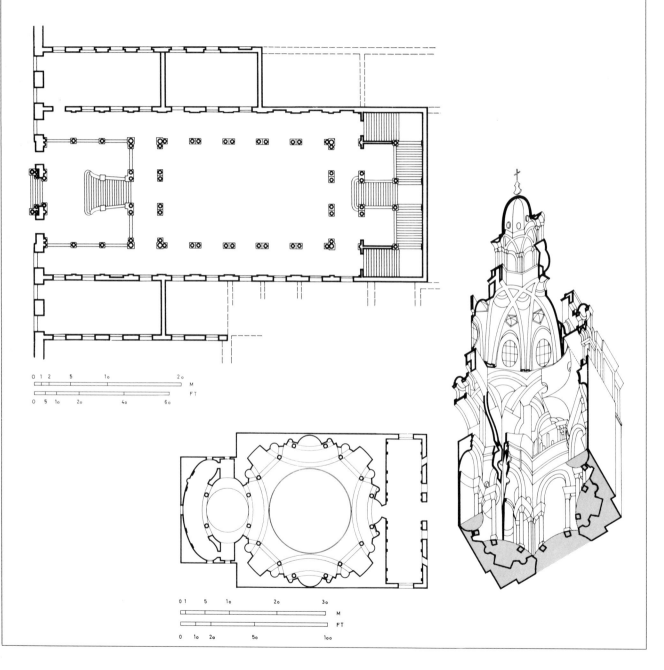

0 1 2   5   1o   2o   M

0 5 1o   2o   4o   6o   FT

0 1   5   1o   2o   3o   M

0 1o 2o   5o   1oo   FT

1. Historical Background

In 1770, when the destructive tide of Neo-Classic art swept across Europe forty years in advance of Napoleon's armies, a relatively uniform Baroque empire stretched from Sicily to Lithuania, embracing Italy, German Switzerland, Austria, Bohemia and Moravia, Roman Catholic Germany and a few pockets of Lutheran territory, and Poland. It also possessed some far-flung outposts such as St Petersburg and the Flemish cities, home ground of Rubens. This empire had a vaguely defined relationship with the Spanish-American countries. European Baroque would indeed have never come into being without the Spanish sixteenth century, its frenzied desire to safeguard the Church, and its passionate love of imagery. Nevertheless, having imparted a few fundamental religious principles to other Catholic nations, and to some extent restored their spiritual outlook, Spain at the start of the seventeenth century turned inwards

Map showing the spread of Baroque in Europe

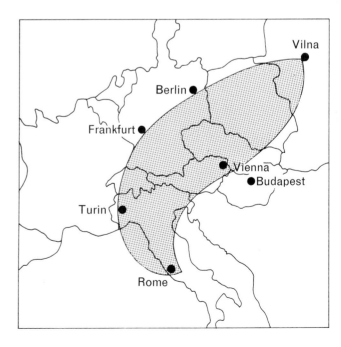

upon herself. Spanish Baroque developed with a rhythm of its own.

The reign of Urban VIII

The rich but fragile empire of Italian and central European Baroque which was eclipsed as suddenly as that of the Incas, was formed in successive waves over a span of one hundred and fifty years, originating in Rome in the second quarter of the sixteenth century. Fifty years later it had spread through the territories of the Danube and in the eighteenth century its center of gravity moved yet further northwards. After 1720, all the major Baroque architects were German.

Baroque is now seen as the art of the Church Triumphant, born of the victorious fervor of the Counter-Reformation. Indeed in 1624, when the newly crowned Pope Urban VIII commissioned Bernini to design the façade of S Bibiana and the Baldacchino for St Peter's, the Jesuits and the Papal Nuncio were engaged on the destruction of Bohemia, one of the strongest bastions of protestant Europe. This trend was soon reversed, however. Ten years after the battle of the White Mountain, Tilly, one of the conquerors of the Czechs, was routed by Gustavus Adolphus, and the Swedes became masters of Germany. The power of the Dutch was in the ascendant, while that of the Hapsburgs began to wane. Baroque was initially the art of Rome at peace amid the storm of a Europe torn by conflict; Rome was profoundly conscious of her destiny, isolated among nations which were either lapsing into decadence or emerging in a welter of violence. Spain's dominating grip was loosening, the Emperor had to keep watch against the heretics in the North, France still had not achieved spiritual unity and laid no claim to leadership. Rome, by contrast, was experiencing a second Renaissance, less as the capital of Christendom reunited than as an oasis of confidence and certainty. She was once again the intellectual and artistic leader of Italy just as she had been in the time of Julius II and Leo X.

Baroque began in a revival of tradition. The twisted columns of the cloisters of S Paolo-fuori-le-Mura and those of the old Basilica of St Peter's, now enclosed in Michelangelo's massive casing, achieve a symbolic enlargement in Bernini's Baldacchino. The real discovery made by Bernini and his contemporary, Pietro da Cortona, in their capacity as architects, was a type of Roman majesty distilled from history and legend. One should not be deceived by their as yet discreet taste for curves nor by the liberties they sometimes took with classic orders. Despite any appearance to the contrary, the climate in which they worked was that which retained Poussin and the classicist sculptor, Duquesnoy, far from their native land. Rather than being fascinated by the Mannerism of Lombardy or Florence, or by a pious functionalism, starkly symbolized by the bare nave of the Gesù Church, these two young men were haunted by the vision of the Antique that had inspired Bramante, Michelangelo, and their great predecessor, Maderno.

The death of Urban VIII in 1644 did not compromise the religious achievement of the Counter-Reformation. The Church was established almost entirely in accordance with the dictums of the Spanish theologians in the Papal Council. The Pope, however, had recovered his status as a formidable – and colorful – temporal ruler, and the artists in his employ were once more preparing to teach Europe the rules of a monumental art.

Innocent X and Alexander VII

Already Baroque was taking new stylistic forms. In Venice, the Church of the Salute was beginning to take shape, and in Genoa rose tiered palaces with staircases and colonnades. These buildings bore little relation to the abstract

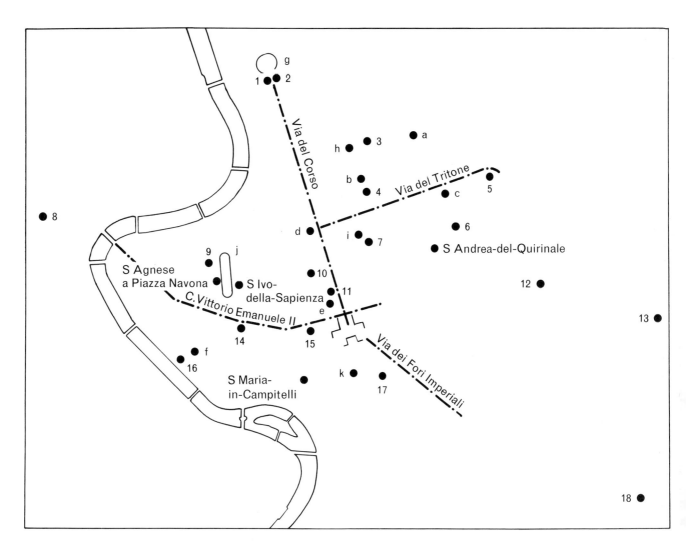

Location of major Baroque churches in Rome

1	S Maria-dei-Miracoli	10	S Ignazio	a	Palazzo Ludovisi
2	S Maria di Monte Sano	11	S Maria-in-Via-Lata	b	Palazzo di Propaganda Fide
3	Trinità-dei-Monti	12	S Maria Maggiore	c	Palazzo Barberini
4	S Andrea-delle-Fratte	13	S Bibiana	d	Palazzo Chigi
5	S Susanna	14	S Andrea-della-Valle	e	Palazzo Doria
6	S Carlo-alle-Quattro-Fontane	15	Gesu	f	Palazzo Farnese
7	SS Vincenzo-ed-Anastasio	16	S Maria-della-Morte	g	Piazza del Popolo
8	St Peter's	17	SS Luca-e-Martina	h	Piazza di Spagna
9	S Maria-della-Pace	18	S Giovanni-in-Laterano	i	Piazza Fontana di Trevi
				j	Piazza Navona
				k	The Capitol

eloquence of Rome. They blended with the sea and the mountains and exploited the newly discovered resources of theatrical scenery. But, most important of all, Rome saw the rise of Borromini. In 1639 he designed the cloister and tiny Church of S Carlo-alle-Quattro-Fontane – a far cry from the pomp of the Vatican which rose under the guidance of Bernini. Later he became the favorite architect of Innocent X, who commissioned him to rebuild S Giovanni-in-Laterano in the Baroque manner, just as Bernini had transformed St Peter's. This thankless task was not suited to Borromini's genius, which lay beyond a gift for adaptation. Instead of basing his themes on traditional architecture, he evolved them from his own theories. For him a curve was more than a flexible variation or link; it was the basic element of a new world. A revolutionary architecture was born in opposition to classical Baroque, damaging it beyond repair, with the aid of two artists who had moved beyond classical principles – Bernini as sculptor and Pietro da Cortona as painter.

About 1650, Borromini completed S Ivo-della-Sapienza, designed the tower and dome of S Andrea-delle-Fratte and, for a few decisive years, supplanted the Rainaldi in their work on S Agnese in the Piazza Navona. At the same time Pietro da Cortona, whose SS Luca-e-Martina dated from the previous pontificate, was building S Maria-della-Pace and S Maria-in-Via-Lata, while Bernini erected the colonnade of St Peter's and the Palazzo Chigi. After 1660, Bernini completed three churches which were entirely of his own design: S Tomaso in Castel-Gandolfo, S Maria-dell'-Assunzione at Ariccia and S Andrea-del-Quirinale. At this time Borromini built the ponderous, heavily-shadowed façades of the Collegio di Propaganda Fide, and S Carlo-alle-Quattro-Fontane.

1667 saw the death of Borromini and Alexander VII, second in succession to Urban VIII,

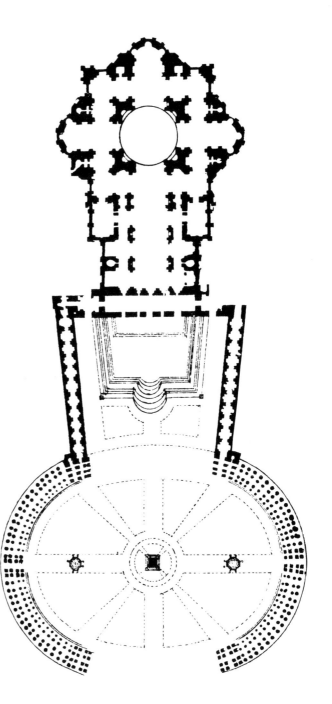

St Peter's, Rome: plan of the basilica fronted by Bernini's colonnade

followed two years later by that of Pietro da Cortona. Although Bernini outlived them, the second Roman Renaissance came to an abrupt end. The city no longer had a privileged part to play in a Europe stabilized by the Treaty of Westphalia and the Pyrenean Treaty, and dominated for the remainder of the century by France. Cardinal Chigi, the Pope's nephew, went to Fontainebleau to apologize for his fellow Romans who had offended Louis XIV's ambassador. Urban VIII's outstretched arm blessed and dominated the world from the summit of his tomb, whereas Alexander VII's tomb shows us a man on his knees facing death in solitude.

A well-practised academism rooted in the preceding period, held sway over the city for more than half a century. Carlo Fontana, the leading architect of the time, reduced Bernini's noble plans to formulae and made clever use of the convex and concave designs of the 1660's. Vitality and imagination found their only outlet in the frescoes of Gaulli and Pozzo which struck the last blow for the Roman Seicento by invading the long vaults of the churches of the Counter-Reformation. In this way the austerity of the Gesù Church was incorporated into the Baroque empire.

Turin

No sooner had Rome fallen into eclipse than a second Baroque capital rose in the North. A few months before Borromini's death, Guarino Guarini, who without actually being his pupil, had most accurately assimilated his ideas, settled in Turin, where he built S Lorenzo and the Cappella della SS Sindone. He belonged to the Theatines, one of the most learned and exclusive orders of the time, whose beliefs were the same as the Reformists and the Jesuits. He was an intellectual, whereas the great Romans, including Borromini, had been marble workers and stonemasons. Nor was he identified with any particular place. It is mere chance that his name

should be indissolubly linked with Turin; his churches at Messina and Lisbon have been destroyed by earthquakes, and the one he built in Paris was pulled down by the Restoration in the nineteenth century. His art possesses a free and unlimited power as did the mathematics he taught and which inspired him. He was as contemptuous of 'styles' as Frank Lloyd Wright, relying rather on a mysterious 'organic' unity to reconcile contradictory components. Without his spectacular daring, the lessons of Borromini might have been lost to Europe, and the influence of Rome might have become identified with Bernini's most assured successes. Thanks to his journeys abroad, his writings and his widespread connections – he sent a design to Prague in 1679 – Guarini taught the future Baroque world that architecture is an exercise in freedom, a means of creating space rather than a commentary on past traditions.

High Baroque

The Baroque of Rome and Piedmont crossed the Alps in the last quarter of the century. In fact, architecture in Germany, Switzerland, Austria and even Poland had long been Italianate. Moreover, the majority of architects were Italian, but the concepts that had penetrated these countries had been discovered and used in Italy long before the time of Bernini and Borromini. This was the great three-aisled basilica with a dome at the point of intersection which Santino Solari introduced at Salzburg in 1614 and which recurs fifty years later in the Theatinerkirche in Munich. The single nave of the Gesù was repeated by the Jesuits at Dillingen on the Danube in 1610, at Vienna and Innsbruck in 1627 and in Solothurn in 1680. Basically traditional buildings, with certain modifications peculiar to their German setting, began to acquire an independent existence, and in their interiors flourished the original decoration known in Germany as High Baroque.

Vaults, entablatures and galleries disappeared beneath the plasterwork reproducing stylized Renaissance motifs and, in some cases, abundant vegetation born of peasant imagination. This frozen tumult of movements often call to mind the wild, frenzied strivings of Spanish Baroque to obliterate the shame of plain surfaces. Yet, paradoxically, in a church like Obermachtel, High Baroque presents a near masterpiece of harmony, a rough form of classicism.

Between 1670-1680, a second wave from Italy passed over the Hapsburg territories of the Holy Roman Empire, bringing with it the fruits of structural research carried out since 1630. The Danube territories had now forgotten the nightmare of the Thirty Years' War. The Treaty of Westphalia had not given the Catholics the triumph they had hoped for at the time of the Battle of the White Mountain. It had practically reduced the Empire to a symbol status, but on the other hand it had lent weight to the hereditary territories of the emperor. Within twenty-five years Prague and Vienna were to become the capitals of European Baroque.

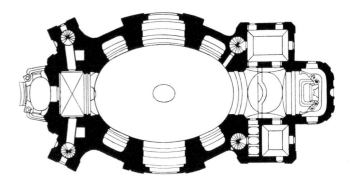

St Peter's, Vienna:
plan by Lukas von Hildebrandt (after Koepf)

Prague

The new rulers, spiritual and temporal, settled in Prague. The homes of the nobility (whom war and Imperial favors had provided with land in Bohemia and Moravia) transformed the Mala Strana, the quarter made fashionable by Wallenstein; starting in 1669, Caratti produced a heavy pastiche of a Bernini façade for the palace of Count Czernin. It was, however, an Italianized Frenchman, J. B. Mathey, who ensured the success of the new architecture by building the Church of the Knights Templar in 1679, and subsequently several palaces including the small suburban palace of Troja. Later, two Germans, Christoph Dientzenhofer and his son, Kilian-Ignaz, gave the city its unique, rather provincial appearance, with its mixture of traditional and revolutionary styles. St Nicholas in Mala Strana, the loveliest of their churches, was topped with a dome in the Roman manner in the mid-eighteenth century after the architects had perfected other innovations. In 1703 some of Guarini's paradoxes were already embodied in

Holy Trinity Church, Salzburg:
plan by Fischer von Erlach (after Koepf)

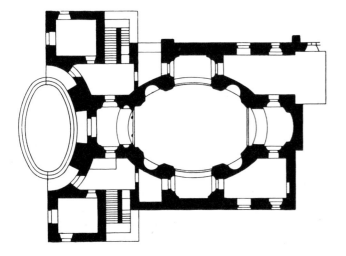

original terms in the nave of the church, the earliest occurrence north of the Alps. The Baroque style matured very quickly in Central Europe, but did not conquer its own capital, Prague, until 1730, when Kilian-Ignaz built the church of St John Nepomuk in the new quarter on the right bank of the Vltava, and a second church of St Nicholas in the Town Hall square, very close to the ancient Tyn church.

Vienna

In 1682, Jan Sobieski repulsed the last wave of Turkish invasion on the Kahlenberg, the Austrains regained the offensive and undertook the reconquest of Hungary. At this historical turning point began the rise of Baroque Vienna,

Karlskirche, Vienna: façade (from a contemporary volume of the works of Fischer von Erlach)

replacing the small Gothic town which had been continually on guard against Turkish attacks. Unlike the quiet city of Prague, Vienna was to become the capital of an international style.

This was promoted by the Italians who drew up plans for the Liechtenstein and Lobkowitz palaces immediately after the Turkish camp had been broken. They were succeeded by Fischer von Erlach, born in 1656, and Lukas von Hildebrandt, born in 1668, both trained in Italy. Both had designed buildings in the provinces; and Von Erlach had proved his mastery of religious architecture in 1694 with the Holy Trinity Church and the University Church in Salzburg. But is was the first twenty years of the eighteenth century that saw the peak of their parallel and rival careers in Vienna. In the center of the city Fischer designed the palace of Prince Eugene, the Batthyany-Schönborn palace, the Bohemian Chancellery, the Trautson palace and the Imperial Library. Hildebrandt built the Church of St Peter and the Kinsky palace whose narrow façade, a concentrated version of that of the Palazzo Chigi, is almost overwhelmed by its windows and pilasters. He also built more spacious palaces at an hour's coach ride from the city for the Schwarzenbergs, Schönborns and Starhembergs, and for Prince Eugene. This new city lacked a church worthy of it; Fischer built the triumphant façade of the Karlskirche opposite the ramparts as a thanksgiving for the disappearance of the plague along with many other fears and phantoms.

Versailles was suffering a temporary eclipse. The treaty of Utrecht and the death of Louis XIV gave the Hapsburgs a great opportunity. The Empire seemed to produce a great outpouring of artistic talent. Italy and Germany met in Vienna. Pozzo came there to paint his frescoes and teach the final discoveries of Roman Baroque relating to perspective. Leibniz stayed there shortly afterwards, and in 1713 dedicated the 'Monadologie' to Prince Eugene. In Leibniz' eyes, it was imperial grandeur that exalted the architecture of Fischer von Erlach. In 1650 it had been Baroque that enabled Rome to look back over the Renaissance and rediscover the traditions of Augustan Rome. In 1715, it helped Vienna to become a new Rome, lending it the presence which the French and German kings formerly expected of the Papacy. Apart from being the ex-voto of a pious prince, the Karlskirche was also an evocation of Trajan's forum, with its famous column and the dome of S Maria-di-Loreto.

Austria and Bohemia

The art of Baroque was at once imperial and close to simple people. Victor L. Tapié has shown that, in Central Europe at least, Baroque had close links to a feudal rural society and an economy based on the traditional exploitation of the great estates. While Fischer and Hildebrandt were setting the scene for a victorious monarchy in Vienna, other architects were at work in country houses and monasteries in the provinces, adapting small churches to the demands of the religious peasant population.

J. Santini-Aichel, a germanized Italian, who was roughly contemporary with Hildebrandt, demonstrated that such a task would admit of no concessions by weaving esoteric variations on themes of Borromini's and Guarini in the region of Prague and, especially, Brno. A country chapel could be more the object of mathematical experiments than folklore and could equally serve as pretext for essays in erudition. Aichel's work was derivative, yet original, since he drew on the Middle Ages rather than Antique models. The vault he desinged at Kladrau makes him a precursor of Viollet-le-Duc, and the ribbed vault at Saar seems pure decoration. At Smirice, however, which was built in 1699, early in his career, these ribs underline the system of thrusts and reveal a profound comprehension of Gothic building, plus a remarkable gift for translating it into the modern idiom.

Prandtauer and Munggenast, architects of the Danube valley, bypassed Aichel's obsession with regeneration and his study of vaults. They adopted without question the Italian pre-Baroque churches as their prototypes. Their magnificent monastic foundations of St Florian, Melk, Zwettl and Dürnstein made a very real contribution to an art which was restricting itself increasingly to religious orders. The great abbeys of Upper and Lower Austria, however, though as wealthy and hospitable as the land from which they sprang, were strangely resistant to change. Their rather oppressive opulence stood fast throughout the Rococo period when even Vienna became susceptible to certain Western influences, the cult of dynasty. With their huge, useless 'Kaiser-Säle,' their empty royal apartments, their vast ostentatious furniture (like the bed at St Florian surrounded by turbaned prisoners ready to guard the sleeping Prince Eugene), their Escorial-like proportions, they continue to mirror, with provincial fidelity, the dreams of grandeur formed at the time of the Treaty of Passarowitz.

Italy in the eighteenth century

While Central Europe found its final rôle in the midst of the Baroque world, there were signs of renewed activity in the South. In 1714, Filippo Juvarra settled in Turin, by mere chance, as was the case with Guarini. Having studied in Rome under the classicist Carlo Fontana, and already attracted the Emperor's attention, this thirty-six year old Sicilian had no particular connections with Piedmont. He drew on no single tradition, but on all. Guarini's world was too personal to have any roots, Juvarra's was the vital crossroads of the eighteenth century. One can detect a French influence in his secular designs, a German one in his religious buildings.

Northern Baroque was clearly becoming an influence in its turn. The basilica of Superga which dominates Turin is a mixture of reminiscences of the Roman style and visions of the future Neo-Classicism. Its silhouette, however, evokes the churches which rise on their promontories above the Danube, joined only by their apses to the massive bulk of the monastery buildings.

While this eclectic master was carrying this style to all the courts of Europe, organizing the

Design for decoration, by Juvara

funeral decorations for Leopold Hapsburg and Peter of Braganza, and adapting it to the tastes of Spain, Vittone the Piedmontese was continuing Guarini's experiments for the benefit of laborers and nuns in isolated communities. Once more stone was put to the service of an all-powerful, imaginative geometry. In 1738, a rich landowner in Carignano commissioned Vittone to build a chapel at Valinotto for his farm laborers. His design emerged unexpectedly as the ultimate heir to Borromini's churches and S Lorenzo in Turin, mingling mathematical equations and the pastoral element characteristic of the Rococo.

Rome, too, came to life again during the pontificates of Benedict XIII and Clement XII (1724-1740). This time there were no innovations, however; it was a matter of accomplishing noble and delightful landscaping – such as the steps of the Piazza di Spagna, the Piazza S Ignazio and the Fontana di Trevi. The city no longer looked outwards to Europe, but took pleasure in itself alone. This was a period when the subtle charm of Valvassori and Raguzzini brought fleeting smiles to Bramante's Rome, and blended with the classicist variations of Fuga and Galilei. It is hard to believe that the Palazzo Doria and the façade of S Giovanni-in-Laterano are exactly contemporary. In her Indian summer, Rome was the only city where a colonnade did not become monotonous, where repetition seemed a charming refrain and where a hint of pastiche was as emotive as a delayed echo. But already S Maria-della-Morte, one of the last churches of the period, was rising in the shadow of the Palazzo Farnese, with a façade whose dull and feeble repetition of the triumphant façades of the Seicento indicates that the springs of Baroque were beginning to run dry.

Meanwhile Naples came into its own, though Baroque underwent no sudden development here. In the city and its surroundings, Charles III, the Bourbon king (1734-59), introduced an international style, a palatial Baroque which achieved its finest expression in Vanvitelli's Caserta. In Sicily and Apulia however, a local Baroque style had been building up a hoard of strange riches over the years; although it derived in part from Rome, its essence was Spanish. In Palermo and Lecce, the eighteenth century was not a clearly defined period, but rather a moment of reckoning. The most original creations of this timeless art are the famous Sicilian villas, notably that of the Prince of Palagonio, where, in 1715, while European nobility were dreaming of Versailles, its owner was collecting monsters.

Germany : the framework

The most exciting development of eighteenth-century Baroque, however, took place between the Alps and the Main, an essentially agricultural region divided into great estates. German Baroque was far less tied to the cities that that of Austria or Czechoslovakia. The old towns of the Empire remained unresponsive to the new architecture. Large cities such as Ulm and Nuremberg, and smaller towns like Reutlingen and Memmingen did in fact largely rally to the Reform, but this was apparently another aspect of the same phenomenon, another manifestation of the same mentality. Moreover, Roman Catholic cities such as Munich, Passau and Würzburg, though they welcomed Baroque, especially if introduced by their Princes, produced scarcely any first-rate religious architecture. The streets of Bamberg are as charming as the Mala Strana, but the town's Baroque churches are merely of historical value. Fulda proudly considers itself a Baroque town, but this is due only to the abbey and its surrounding buildings.

The fragmentary political division of Germany had a lot to do with this. Every petty prince wanted to have his own Versailles and Marly. Nevertheless, it is rather a sweeping

Map of Bavaria showing major Baroque sites mentioned in the text

1 Benrath	13 Wiblingen	25 Ottobeuren
2 Brühl	14 Günzburg	26 Kempten
3 Fulda	15 Dillingen	27 Wies
4 Bamberg	16 Weltenburg	28 Wessobrunn
5 Pommersfelden	17 Regensburg	29 Diessen
6 Nuremberg	18 Rohr	30 Fürstenfeld
7 Käppel	19 Osterhofen	31 Altomünster
8 Waldsassen	20 Passau	32 Schleissheim
9 Dresden	21 St Blasien	33 Rott-am-Inn
10 Bruchsal	22 Birnau	34 Altötting
11 Ludwigsburg	23 Salem	
12 Stuttgart	24 Weingarten	

varied from state to state. There was an uneasy balance between these imported elements and the rich local heritage of Gothic architecture and late medieval sculpture. The value of the German eighteenth century lies partly in these hesitations, subtle choices, second thoughts, which are laid bare in successive plans for Würzburg castle or for important churches such as Ottobeuren and Vierzehnheiligen.

The estates of the Schönborn family saw a rigorous exchange of influences; here flourished an art whose elements drew on East, West and South, yet it was the opposite of eclectic. In Vienna, the Schönborns had achieved high imperial honors. Their Rhineland bishoprics, and the Electorate of Mainz in particular, now put them in contact with France. The bishopric of Bamberg bordered on the Slav world. This loose collection was inspired by similar ideas based on a passion for great architecture, but each separate territory retained the ability to elaborate its individual formula.

In the Schönborns, the episcopate had the most outstanding patrons of the day, but it was their traditional enemies, the monks, who dominated German Baroque. They also enjoyed complete autonomy. Numerous abbeys, especially in Swabia and Switzerland, were subject to no temporal authority. These included the 154 Benedictine houses in the German lands, among them St Blasien, Fulda, St Emmeram at Regensburg, Kempten, whose abbots were princes of the Empire, St Gallen, Einsiedeln, Disentis, Muri, Ochsenhausen, Ottobeuren, Neresheim and Weingarten. Others again owed allegiance to the Premonstratensians, the Augustinian Canons and Cistercians. The great monasteries which were subject to a particular prince often negotiated with him as an equal. Zwiefalten bought its independence from the Duke of Würtemberg in 1750, while Fürstenfeld acted as the Duke of Bavaria's bankers. The

assumption to suggest that each copied Versailles. The very multiplicity of states allowed the penetration of diverse influences and provoked a series of original freaks. The proportion of Italian and French influence, or rather of 'Imperial Baroque' transmitted by Austria, and the Guarini influence from Bohemia and Moravia

abbots, in the main commoners, ruled over their few thousand subjects with as much patriotism and often with more wisdom than their lay counterparts. The only temptation to which they were prey seems to have been architecture. They were not only tempted by fame, but by the knowledge that such buildings were a speculative investment. New ones would attract the faithful and bring in the donations. This did not apply so much to the monastery buildings which often bore witness to overwhelming wealth and power, as to the pilgrim churches where the people felt at home worshipping close to the holy images. The Cistercians of Salem built the Church of Birnau to divert the faithful from the neighboring town of Uberlingen, and those of Langheim undertook the building of Vierzehnheiligen on condition that the Bishop of Bamberg allowed them to keep almost the total revenue from the offerings over the next ten years. Pilgrims at Andechs, after kneeling before the Virgin, eagerly drank beer brewed in the monastery, and even today the monks preside over the fairs which swell their income.

German architects

The turn of the century saw the rise of the Dientzenhofer family in Franconia near the Bohemian frontier. They brought to Germany the Roman Baroque which had swept the Hapsburg domains thirty years earlier about 1670. The eldest brother Georg, uncle of the Prague Dientzenhofers, built the pilgrim church of Käppel in 1689; another brother, Johann, was recalled from Rome in 1699 to rebuild the abbey church of Fulda. He made few innovations on the traditional basilica, apart from erecting a variation on the Baldacchino of St Peter's at the entrance to the choir. The rhythmic, fluid structure of Banz however, which dates from 1710, shows a sudden return to the style of Guarini. In the same year Dientzenhofer built the model of all Baroque palaces, Pommersfelden, for the Elector Lothar-Franz von Schönborn.

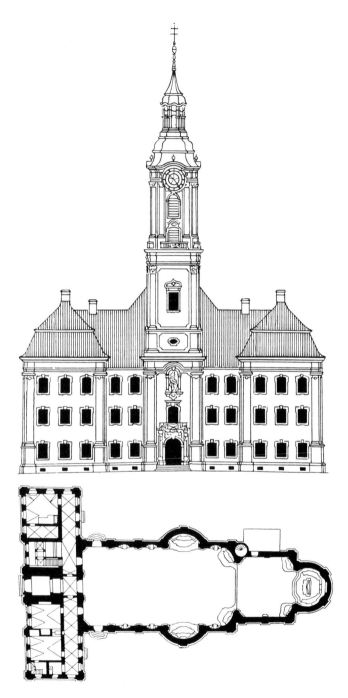

Birnau: façade and plan of church by Peter Thumb (after Koepf)

It was the age of palaces. In Berlin the residence of the future Prussian monarchy was nearing completion; in Dresden, Pöppelmann was building the Zwinger; the building of Ludwigsburg had begun. The Treaty of Utrecht brought financial optimism and a certain number of German princes back to their courts. The Elector Max-Emmanuel returned to Bavaria, began Schleissheim and employed the classicist Effner to take up work at Nymphenburg. Shortly afterwards, Bishop Philipp-Franz von Schönborn started the palace at Würzburg, one of the most imprtant buildings of the period, and Cardinal Schönborn, Prince Bishop of Speyer, commenced his own at Bruchsal.

About 1720 a generation of outstanding church architects were beginning work. The brothers Asam, Dominikus Zimmermann, Johann-Michael Fischer, Peter Thumb, and Balthazar Neumann were all born between 1680 and 1695. They took over from the Italian architects responsible for the plans, leaving the German master-masons and the masters of the old guilds in charge of directing operations.

Cosmas Damian and Egid-Quirin Asam must be studied separately. Firstly, from a chronological point of view, their first important buildings, Rohr and Weltenburg, date from 1717, clearly preceding those of their contemporaries. Secondly, because Cosmas Damian was primarily a painter, Egid-Quirin a sculptor, they did not approach building in the meditative way of Johann Dientzenhofer at Banz. What they brought back from Rome, fifteen years after Dientzenhofer, was the sculptural style of Bernini, together with echoes of the great frescoes of the late Seicento and the epic perspective of Brother Pozzo. From these elements they created interior space, or, in other words, architecture. This is clearly seen at Osterhofen where their altarpieces, their sculptured groups and painted walls distract attention from what is

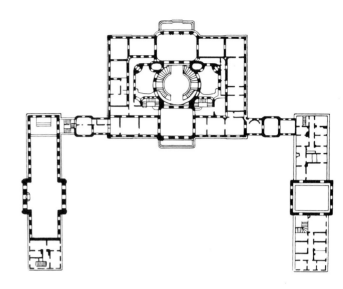

Bruchsal Castle: plan, by von Welsch, von Grünstein and Neumann (after Koepf)

a traditional structure. It is also apparent at St John Nepomuk, built in 1753 as a private chapel for Egid-Quirin's house.

The Asam brothers proved their originality in another way, due doubtless to their loyalty to Rome and their 'expressive' conception of interior decoration: this was their resistance to Rococo which swamped Germany after 1730. This was, without doubt, France's greatest contribution to contemporary architecture, apart from the classicism which emanated from Versailles. The spellbinding subtlety of this rich, abstract decoration emerged, as the reign of Louis XIV was drawing to its close, to rule supreme during the Regency, then fell into disfavor in the Paris of Madame de Pompadour. Now it was instantly absorbed to perfection by the artists in Germany. In Munich, it produced the Amalienburg, and transformed the churches.

This was largely the victory of the art of

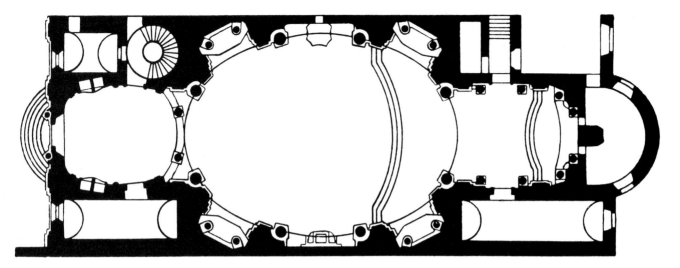

Weltenburg: plan by the Asam Brothers (after Koepf)

Günzburg: Church of Our Lady, plan by Zimmermann
(after Koepf)

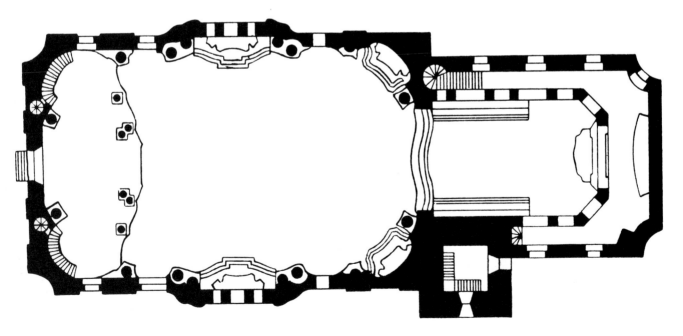

stucco, and hence of its greatest practitioners —
the villagers of Wessobrunn in Upper Bavaria
where the craft had long been taught to perfection. Under Dominikus Zimmermann, Wessobrunn for the first time became a creative
force on its own account. As might be expected
from a village in the century that produced
Favart, it dreamed up idylls, such as Steinhausen, Günzburg and Wies, perhaps the only
dreams that have not turned stale after two
hundred years. Günzburg is a pink and gold
parish church; Wies is still the most famous
Bavarian pilgrim church. Zimmermann died
there, having made of it the sum of his experience. To some, its setting in a circle of pine
trees may seem rather theatrical, too reminiscent of folk art; they may prefer Steinhausen,
the church which is the center of the Swabian
village life. One must hear a peasant congregation singing mass during Holy Week in the nave
of this church, with its pastel colors and frescoes
full of thickets, gushing streams and wild
animals, to reach a true appreciation of the
Rococo.

Zimmermann and Egid-Quirin Asam worked
in different styles, though both were craftsmen
in stucco. J. M. Fischer's speciality lay in
stone and brick. He worked his way up in the
Munich Guild of Masons and gained his knowledge of Italian methods while working in the
Moravian building yards. 32 churches and 23
monasteries to his credit make him the most
prolific architect of his generation. His style
was, however, uneven, since he conformed to the
needs, resources and traditions of the houses
whose abbots employed him. At Osterhofen in
1726, at Diessen in 1732 and at Zwiefalten in
1740, he provided the supports for magnificent
decorations. By experimenting with perspective
effects already well known in Southern Germany,
he carried to its furthest extreme the sceno-
graphic Baroque that had originated in Venice.
The church of Ottobeuren, built in the fifties,

expresses the power of an ancient Benedictine
abbey, financially and politically independent,
uniting imperial grandeur and the Rococo. At
the more modest abbey of Rott-am-Inn (1759),
on the other hand, the richness is one of
structural complexity. Altomünster, his last
building, is also the most difficult to interpret,
because the monks, lay brothers, nuns and
parishioners of this Brigittine community had to
occupy separate areas of the church; visual
connections have to effect a sense of unity in
the resulting succession of areas and tiered
galleries.

Peter Thumb was also the heir to a collective
family tradition, that of Vorarlberg. The master-
masons of Vorarlberg were the only ones to
challenge the Italians in Germany and Switzerland in the seventeenth century, and provided
High Baroque decoration with its most suitable
setting. Michael Thumb, Peter's father, built
Obermachtel. Their fellow countryman, Moos-

Rott-am-Inn: convent church, section and plan
by Fischer (after Koepf)

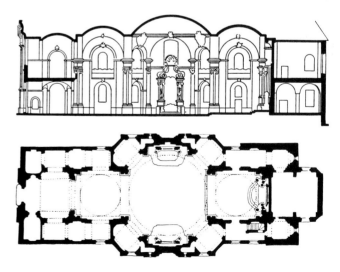

brugger, after building Muri and Disentis, worked at Weingarten about 1715 before realizing his most important achievement at Einsiedeln. In his turn, Peter Thumb divided his activities between Swabia and Switzerland: in the former he built the last of the pilgrim churches at Birnau, and in the latter he erected the last of the great abbeys, St Gallen.

Balthazar Neumann, the architect of the Schönborns was a foundry worker when an officer of the Würzburg garrison taught him mathematics and turned him into a military engineer. He traveled all over the Empire, visited Vienna and Milan, and came to Paris in 1723 to submit his plans for the palace of Würzburg to Robert de Cotte and Boffrand; his training was as balanced as the taste of his Schönborn employers. Successor to Hildebrandt and Dientzenhofer, and hence to Guarini, he instigated more research into building techniques than any other German architect. He had dreams simultaneously of classical precepts, columns clearly free-standing and aligned in the French manner. He spurned ornament, using his little church at Etwashaven to produce an amazing example of unadorned Baroque, a sort of intellectual Rococo. He was much less tied to the monasteries than Fischer; he designed the palace at Werneck, played a decisive role in the building of Würzburg and Brühl, and erected pilgrim churches independent of any monastery, like Käppel and Gössweinstein. He designed Vierzehnheiligen for the abbey of Langheim in 1744, without the support of the abbot who was indifferent to his great European style and only tolerated it under the constraint of his bishop. Circumstances forced him into a compromise to which we owe the most original church in Germany. At the end of his life he left the valleys of the Main and Rhine for the Swabian monasteries where he worked harmoniously with the abbot of Neresheim to produce a church which was the sum of all his aspirations.

The advent of Neo-Classicism

The classical dream which Neumann was unable to realize at Vierzehnheiligen was brought to life in caricature by the decorators of Neresheim. About 1750 there was a shortage of funds for stucco-work and altars which were not completed until the Winckelmann era.

By 1770, the great architects of the Rococo were dead, and their successors were under the same compulsion as painters and sculptors to draw their inspiration from the Antique. There was, at best, a certain Louis XVI charm to be found amid the garlands and urns, to appease the nostalgia of the viewer. In 1773, Michael d'Ixnard of Nîmes designed an elegant, discreetly worldly church for the noble nuns of Buchau. Although tradition ascribes it to Rococo, it stems more clearly from the German 'Aufklärung;' its grace and good taste are purely secular, well-mannered 'putti,' very distant relations of the ecstatic cherubs of the great period of Wessobrunn, adorn the confessionals. Such successes were few and most churches gave way before a cold Neo-Classicism. Rot-an-der-Rot, built in 1784, is a phantom mausoleum of Baroque forms and styles – a Baroque church without a soul.

The end of the Baroque coincided with a reaction against the monasteries. The German rulers began to try to limit their power and independence. These events were forerunners of the secularizations of 1803. Less than a generation after the deaths of Fischer and Peter Thumb, that Central Europe born of the Treaty of Westphalia, the delicate, old-fashioned, irrational support of Baroque, was crumbling. The Empire, in 1648 a mere empty symbol which Baroque civilization had in part revitalized, vanished beneath an attack from the West that flourished on the anti-Baroque myths of Nature, Reason and the Antique.

Plates

Prague

67 **St Nicholas in Mala Strana.** The apse with the dome and tower, and part of the district of Mala Strana, from the north-east. The spire on the left belongs to the church of St Thomas. In the background are the wooded slopes which contain the Vrtbov Palace gardens, and, further west, those of the Lobkovic.

68 The west façade. The flanking bays are concave. The central bay has an outward curve, stressed by coupled columns and pilasters, but interrupted at the centre by a contrary movement. This undulating line is a direct evocation of the façade of S Carlo-alle-Quattro-Fontane.

69 North side of the nave. Note the placing of the piers, whose diagonals are parallel to the axis of the nave, in accordance with the precepts of Guarini, and the undulating galleries.

Saar

70 **St John Nepomuk on the Green Hill.** Façade. The main door opens into one of the five elliptical chapels forming a necklet round the central space.

71 The central gallery and dome. At the bottom of the illustration in the center, is one of the 'points' which functions as a choir. The pentagonal design is repeated at each level.

Melk

72 **The Abbey.** The monastery building from the west.

74 The spur overlooking the Danube. The façade of the church between the ends of the wings of monastery buildings.

75 The principal courtyard of the Abbey.

76 Looking up the façade of the church.

77 North side of the nave. Compare with plate 69. The nave is bounded by a richly ornamented, yet solid, wall. The pilasters stand all aligned, the entablature is unbroken, and the galleries do not make any real impression.

78 The dome over the crossing, from the left transept.

79 The 'böhmische Kappen,' of the nave. Each bay remains autonomous, but the frescoes are beginning to continue unbroken over the transverse ribs.

Vienna

80 **Karlskirche.** Façade. The width of the nave equals that of the portico, that of the transepts the distance between the two 'Trajan's columns.'

81 The dome.

St Gallen

82 **The Abbey** from the air. The twin-towered façade acts, in fact, as the apse of the church.

83 The Library. A very fine example of a Rococo monastery library (1756-1759).

Einsiedeln

84 **The Abbey.** General view of the façade.

85 The central curve of the façade.

86 Bay of the façade, and details.

87 The octagonal space constituting the first bay of the nave. In the center, the chapel housing the Black Virgin, the goal of the pilgrimage to Einsiedeln.

88 The nave from the pilgrims' assembly area. On the right is the chapel and one of the pillars on to which it backs.

89 The nave, seen from the central area.

90 Summit of the pillar facing the pulpit. The decoration dates from the pre-Rococo phase. The frescoes have expanded, the stuccos are fluid and abstract, but the essay in asymmetry is still uncertain.

St Nicholas in Mala Strana, Prague, by Dientzenhofer
Plan 1:600

St John Nepomuk on the Green Hill, Saar, by Aichel
Plan 1:300

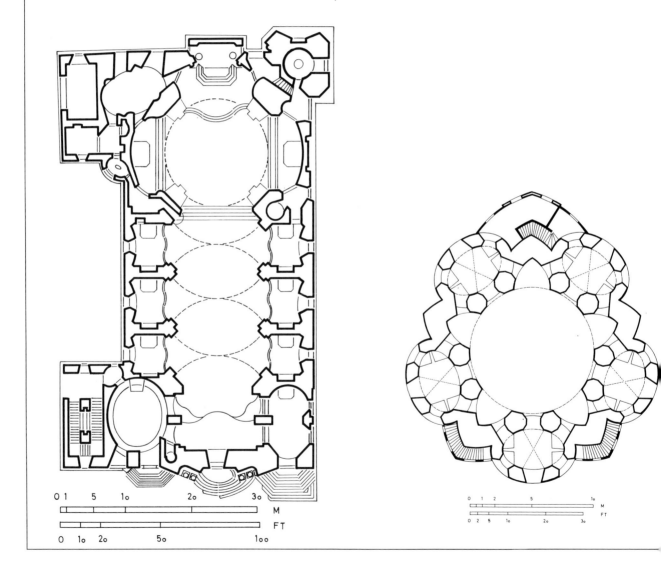

0 1   5   1o   2o   3o
M

FT

0   1o   2o   5o   1oo

0 1 2   5   1o
M
FT
0 2 5   1o   2o   3o

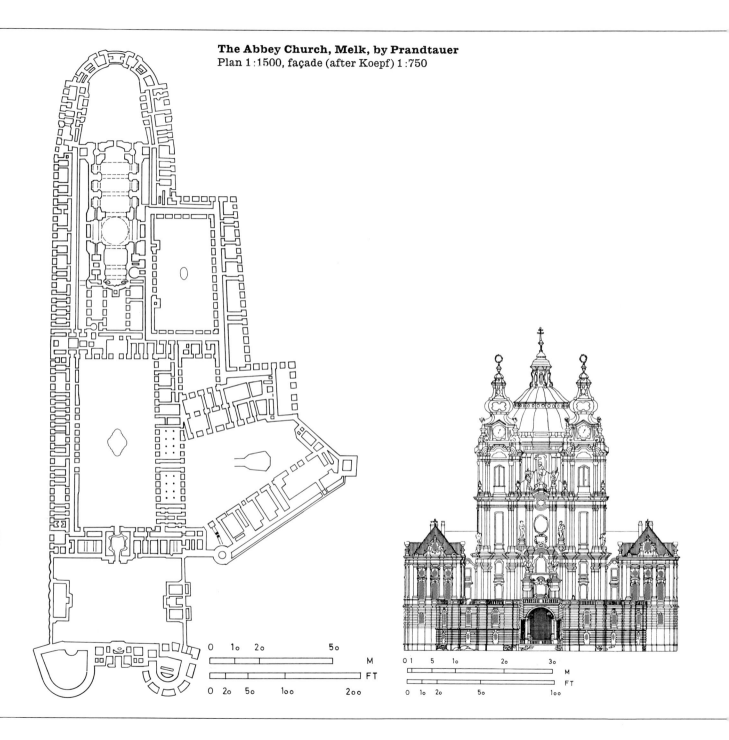

The Abbey Church, Melk, by Prandtauer
Plan 1:1500, façade (after Koepf) 1:750

O   1o   2o   5o
                              M
                              FT
O 2o 5o   1oo   2oo

O 1 5 1o   2o   3o
                              M
                              FT
O 1o 2o   5o   1oo

Notes

Prague

St Nicholas in Mala Strana

The first building period, which produced the façade and the nave, lasted from 1703 to 1711. On the piers of the nave, prolonged by pilasters, Christoph Dientzenhofer set oblique arches joined at the keystones; these divided the vault into a series of ovals separated by coupled triangles (see Banz). In the course of the second building period (1739-1752) Kilian-Ignaz, Christoph's son, abolished the arches and unified the vault which was covered with a great fresco. At the same time, he widened the choir and the arms of the transept, accentuating the central crossing by placing two columns in front of each of the four angle pillars; above it he built a lofty dome with a drum, one of the last of the Baroque era.

Christoph Dientzenhofer (1655-1722) was one of five brothers from Aibling in Upper Bavaria and settled in Prague in 1678. Chief works: Woborischt (1702) St Klara at Eger, and the monastery of Brevnov (1708), the Loreto in Prague (1717). Kilian-Ignaz (1698-1750) built several churches in Prague. Best known are St John-Nepomuk-by-the-Rock (1730) and St Nicholas in the Old Town (1732).

Saar

St John Nepomuk on the Green Hill

In Moravia, on the borders of Bohemia. Built between 1719-1722. Johann Santini-Aichel (1667-1723) was born in Prague of a family of stonecutters who had come from Italy. He restored the Gothic churches of the monasteries at Sedlec (1703) and Kladrau (1712) and built the pilgrim churches of Maria-Teinitz (1711) and Kiritein (1710), the Cistercian abbey of Königsaal (Zbraslav) in 1716, the Thun palace in Prague, the Castle of Karlskrone (Chlumec), and the monastery of Raigern in 1722.

Melk

Abbey Church

Twelfth-century Benedictine foundation, on the Danube, 80 kilometers from Vienna. The monastery buildings were largely built by Prandtauer between 1702 and 1740.

The church (1702-1714) was not finally completed until 1734. J. M. Rottmayr began the frescoes in 1716, assisted by Fanti, an Italian who specialized in architectural 'trompe l'oeil.' Beduzzi erected the high altar about 1730. Prandtauer (1660-1726) was born at Landeck in the Tyrol. He built the pilgrim churches of Maria Taferl and Sonntagberg.

Vienna

Karlskirche

Built by J. B. Fischer von Erlach to fulfil a vow made by Emperor Charles VI during the plague of 1713. Foundation stone laid in 1716. Fischer's son finished the building in 1729. Frescoes by Rottmayr and Fanti.

St Gallen

Abbey Church

Benedictine foundation dating from Carolingian period. Several architects provided plans for the church, including Johann Michael Beer who probably designed the façade. The decisive influence, however, was that of Peter Thumb (1681-1766), master of the guild of masons at Au in Vorarlberg and former assistant to Franz Beer. Work begun in 1755. Stuccos in the nave and rotunda by Christian Wenzinger (1757) in choir by the brothers Gigl (1764). Side altars by F. Sporer (1769). Classical high-altar by J. S. Moosbrugger.

Einsiedeln

Abbey Church

Subject to Benedictine rule since tenth century. Caspar Moosbrugger, a lay brother from Vorarlberg, began the church in 1719. Work completed after his death, in 1735. Its considerable dimensions were: length 339 feet; maximum width 126 feet; height about 120 feet. Frescoes by C. D. Asam. Stuccos and pulpit by E. Q. Asam (1724). Most of the retables are by Josef Anton Feuchtmayer, but those in the center bay have Italian statues and altar-pieces. The pilgrim chapel built by Santino Solari in 1617 on the spot where the hermit Meinrad lived about 860. Destroyed in 1798 by Masséna's troops, and rebuilt in 1815 with the same materials, but to only two-thirds of its former size.

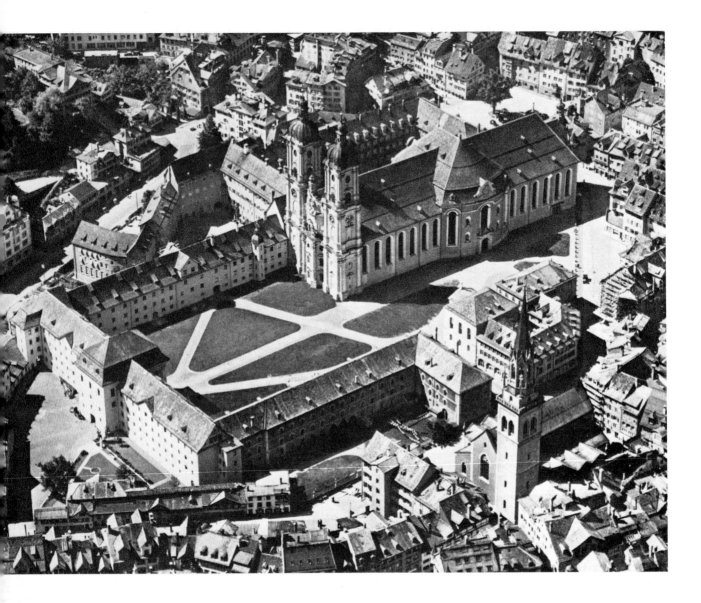

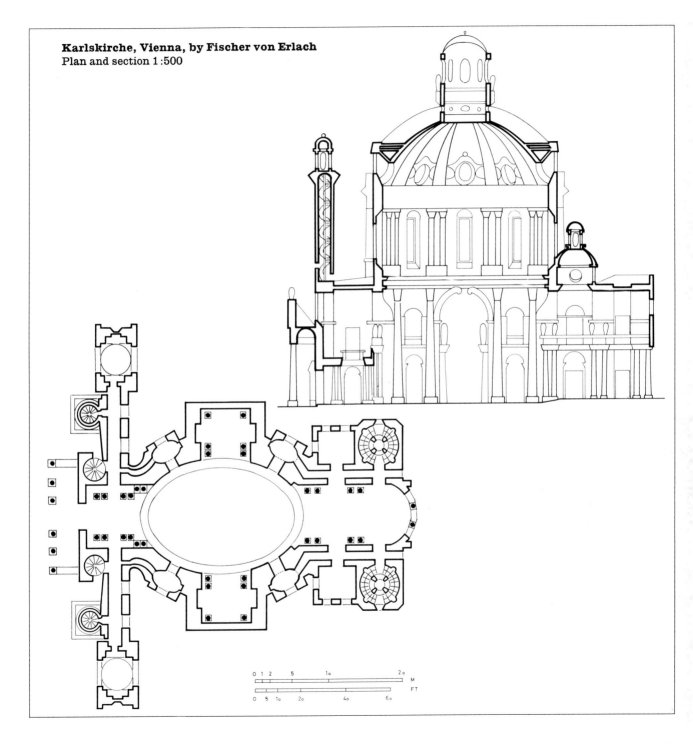

Karlskirche, Vienna, by Fischer von Erlach
Plan and section 1:500

0 1 2   5   1o   2o   M
                          FT
0   5 1o   2o   4o   6o

The Abbey, St Gallen, by Thumb
Plan 1:750

The Abbey Church, Einsiedeln, by Moosbrugger
Plan of the Abbey Church 1:4000; general plan 1:1000

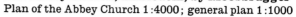

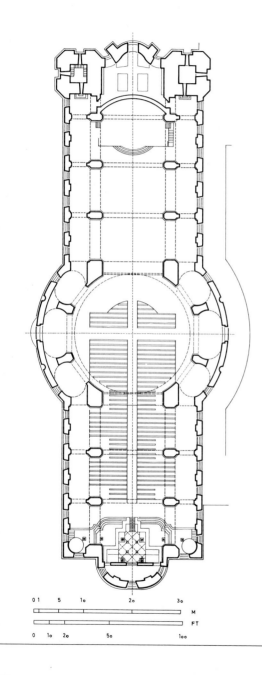

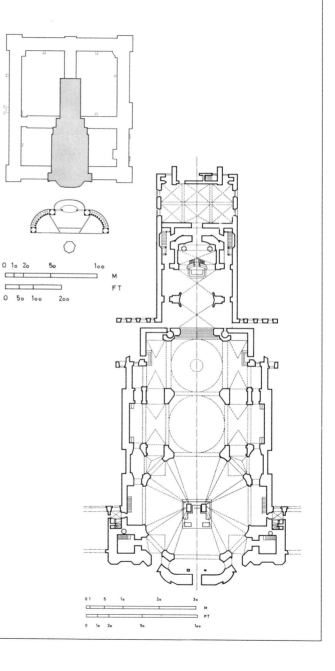

2. Religious Architecture: Plans and Elevations

Plans of Roman Churches

The Counter-Reformation fully restored the significance and prestige of the medieval longitudinal church plan, with its sense of movement towards the altar. At the requests of the Jesuits, among others, Vignole produced an economical version of the Basilica that was not too grandiose. By adding a nave to St Peter's in the seventeenth century, Maderno spectacularly banished the inspiration of Bramante and Michelangelo.

SS Luca-e-Martina, which shows the new architecture, forms an almost perfect Greek cross. Pietro da Cortona set a large dome at the junction of the four arms, to cancel out the nave space and block any sense of movement in it. Judging by the plan, this seems to be a return to the ideal of perfect balance and a refusal to look beyond it. Bernini designed his church at Castel-Gandolfo on a square and his church at Ariccia on a circle, both classical forms. When Borromini took over building S Agnese, he was faced with a Greek cross plan. To increase its originality, he disrupted the longitudinal stress even more drastically than had been foreseen by the Rainaldis. He extended the transverse arms of the cross so that the eye is led away from the high altar to right and left. The area of wall separating the arms was also adjusted, so that Borromini changed the crossing whose area is stressed by the dome, into an exact octagon.

S Ivo's design is based on two intersecting equilateral triangles. The point of one contains the recess of the high altar, that of the other a minute narthex, and the intersecting areas form a sort of hexagonal nave. The ternary rhythm is pronounced – three concave bays whose dominating emphasis attracts the eyes, alternate with three insignificant convex bays. The recess of the high altar is balanced by two recesses which frame the entrance on the opposite side. The curved line of the entrance is balanced by two convex recesses on either side of the altar,

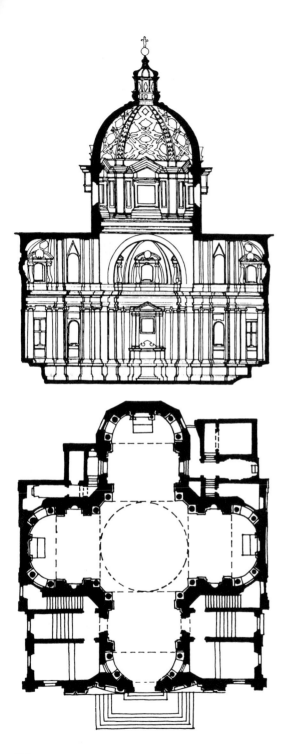

pierced by empty niches which do not hold one's attention. The interlacing triads offer homage to a sacred number, corresponding to the Holy Trinity.

The structure of S Ivo with its beautifully traced cornice at the base of the dome which rises without a break from the nave, does not technically admit of a dominant orientation. Yet, as Wittkower has noted, it in fact conceals a lack of balance which is forced on one's notice, because the hexagon is not perfectly symmetrical. The longitudinal axis links two sides, and the transverse axis, two angles. To right and left, the eye is jarred by two superfluous corners, two awkward intersections. This lays bare the real finality of the Baroque central plan. It is no longer a question of balancing all restlessness. The unity created by these geometrical combinations is not absolute. Borromini merged his two triangles to prevent us from being distracted. Yet there is no response to be found at ground level, as one turns and follows the provoking alternation of pilasters, blank panels and empty niches. The nave which calls up this movement is, in itself, no way out. It is the dome, the sealed cover of Renaissance churches, which here opens a triumphant exit towards the lantern, due to the uninterrupted rise of the ribs between the wide windows.

In S Andrea-del-Quirinale, Bernini fought to minimize the stabilizing transverse axis. By siting the entrance and the high altar on the smaller axis of the ellipse, he seems to have wanted to break all flow of movement, creating a dormant area, like an architect of another age. But the main axis terminates at a blind spot in the wall between the side chapels, so that the eye is led on forwards to the obliquely placed

SS Luca-e-Martina, Rome: section and plan, by Pietro da Cortona

94

altars and then the high altar which is sheltered in an embryo choir framed by a rich portico. It is this choir which gives meaning to S Andrea, just as the dome does to S Ivo. Lacking the depth to form a separate area depriving the church of its central plan unity, it transforms the secondary axis on which it lies into a majestic feature.

In S Carlo-alle-Quattro-Fontane, Borromini combined powerful centralization and pronounced symmetry with an oblong plan. His favorite pair of triangles are here joined at the base, so that the central space is based on the form of a lozenge. The oval dome is placed lengthwise, thus emphasizing the orientation, in contradiction to the transverse axis which is checked by an altar at each point of impact. However, these contradictions are resolved thanks to the supple line of the walls which encircle the extremities of the main axis and the center curve with an undulating movement.

S Maria-in-Campitelli (also known as S Maria-in-Portico), on the other hand, is a right-angled poem. In the eyes of G. C. Argan, it is the first building in the history of architecture to owe nothing to tradition or the architect's imagination. It responds to the needs of an exact program. Rainaldi had to design this church with a mind to the passage and accommodation of crowds of pilgrims, a complex problem which recurs elsewhere. Basically, what he did was to place side by side two central plan systems each consisting of a central space and four subsidiary chapels. A nave in the form of a Greek cross leads to a square choir surmounted by its own dome which lights it separately. This repeated recourse to two Renaissance plans – separating two elements of Bramante's church, width and light from above – results in a long perspective.

Design for altars; color wash, Italian School
(Fatio Collection)

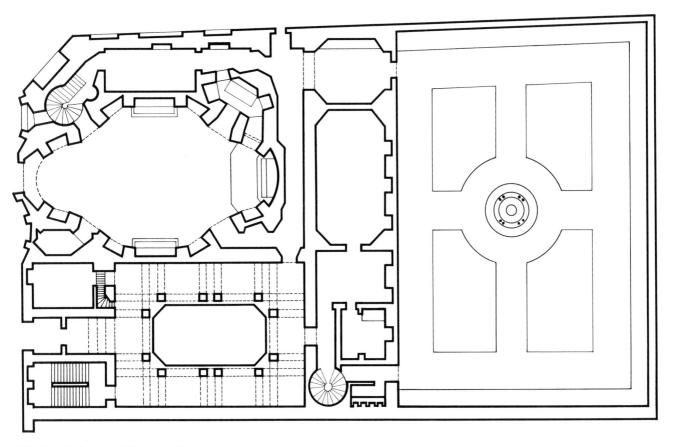

S Carlo-alle-Quattro-Fontane, Rome:
plan of church and cloister, by Borromini

Rome and its façades

By lengthening St Peter and drawing the visitor away from the dome, Maderno was forced to make the façade an independent monument. The first generation of seventeenth-century architects tried to discover an ideal façade for their churches; it was Maderno who, at S Susanna, in 1603, showed most promise of achieving this. The masters of Roman Baroque were to extend the scope of this search, despite their return to the central plan. This was doubtless because they could thus give prominence to one side of the building, proposing an orientation without altering the balance of the interior space. In other words, the façade was a concession. Although in some cases it hinted at a few of the themes developed in the interior, it still gave little idea of the building itself; it was often less the façade of the church itself than of the group of buildings concealing it. Its role was not to be the church's representative, but to set the seal on its integration in a semi-religious, semi-secular complex.

Pietro da Cortona's façade for SS Luca-e-Martina and Borromini's for S Agnese bear witness to this. Both run tangential to the extremities of their naves, only touching them in passing, and exceeding them in width. Cortona uses a post-Tridentine façade of two storeys, but, by making the upper one equal in width to the lower, manages to transform it into a monumental curtain, firmly anchored by ten vertical lines of columns and pilasters, which screens both the theologically suspect Greek cross arrangement and a huddle of sacristies. Borromini has also disguised his plan, but the façade onto the Piazza Navona is far from being a curtain. Its concave line welcomes the visitor, attracting him towards the central portico, and suggesting a movement which is denied by the octagonal nave. Moreover, the dome plays a part in the composition by modifying its function. This chief stabilizing element of the interior structure has to compete on the exterior with two slender, perforated towers and plays its part in creating a brilliant upward movement.

The dome of S Ivo does not form part of a façade but takes the place of one, at least from second storey level. An allusion to the plan of the interior is very perceptible here. The dome is enlarged by the western apses, the key points which balance the high altar; they give it its flowing contours, allowing it to prolong the concave line of the courtyard of the Sapienza and act as counterpoint to it. But its frontality peters out abruptly with the upper storey and the lantern rises uninterrupted in the form of a small temple whose prototype is at Baalbek; this in turn is prolonged by a spiral whose inspiration is Mesopotamian.

At the end of his life, Borromini seems to have reverted to the idea of an autonomous façade. That of S Carlo-alle-Quattro-Fontane may be compared with the two-storeyed rectangle of SS Luca-e-Martina, but bears no resemblance to a curtain. The mask has become ingrained in the body of the church to the full depth of its grooves and cavities, and betrays its convulsions. There are no more plain surfaces; everything has become expressive. The columns, out of proportion with one another, are like statues portraying overwhelming mass and inadequacy. The vegetation on the capitals sprouts in tortured lines, and the lintel of the central niche is a quivering mass of angels' feathers. After a thirty year quest, the face of the Baroque church is emerging at last, unrelated to the one dreamed of by the architect of the white interior of S Carlo in the time of Urban VIII.

Elsewhere, however, the façade as such, as prologue, pursued a more measured development. Pietro da Cortona rounded out the lower storey of S Maria-della-Pace into a hexastyle rotunda, and his façade to S Maria-in-Via-Lata is a building in itself, a two-storeyed loggia forming a narthex. At S Maria-in-Campitelli the bulk typical of Cortona is combined with the traditional scheme of two unequal storeys sometimes linked by volutes, an idea which originated at the Gesù and was used at S Ignazio, S Andrea-della-Valle and many other churches. At SS Vincenzo-ed-Anastasio, opposite the Trevi Fountain, there is a profusion of columns, not to create a series of superimposed tabernacles in the manner of Rainaldi, but to form decorative triads resembling fragments of an organ case.

Longhena

The octagon of the Salute at Venice, with its ambulatory, has the motionless majesty of S Vitale at Ravenna, without the hieratic gold of the latter. On the contrary, it is humanized by the use of soft gray stone, to outline the regular succession of arcades in the manner of Brunelleschi. The chapels on the periphery and those parts of the ambulatory which link them with the nave are quite symmetrical. A heavy crown of windows weighs down the great arches, counteracting the upward thrust of the dome and lessening its power of attraction. Longhena,

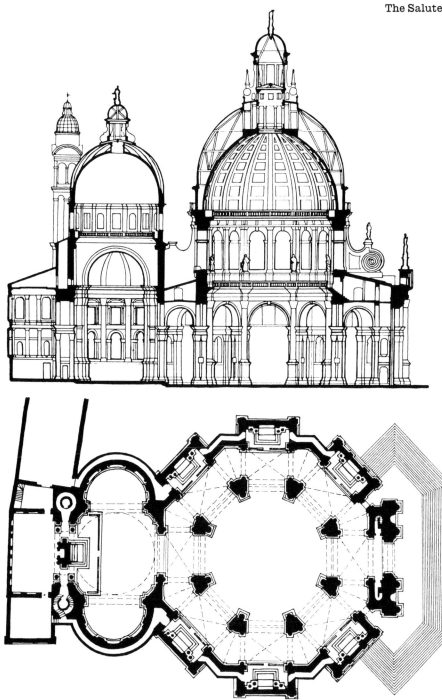

The Salute, Venice: section and plan, by Longhena

however, added a choir to one of the bays. This lent an ethereal quality to the solidity of the design. His perfect rotunda becomes a moving passage, pierced by a perspective at the end of which shines the high altar, framed by three arches whose piers are spaced like the wings of stage scenery. Two bays of the ambulatory and the two small lateral apses of the choir are largely hidden from the visitor as he crosses the threshold. He senses that they stretch like stage wings to right and left of the perspective. It is no longer a clearly defined, almost tangible growth of the nave, as at S Andrea-del-Quirinale, which gives an unbalanced effect here, but an uneven blend of the seen and the half-seen in the neighboring areas. For the first time an architect has built walls which the eye in part rejects, preferring the impression created by their succession and interruptions. In the interior, the optical effects tend to conceal the structure, but the exterior flaunts it with a brilliant freedom foreign to Roman Baroque. The Salute has no façade seen from the Grand Canal; it is clearly defined as a centralized building. The volume borrowed from the façade of the Gesù, swollen and multiplied in three dimensional space, here serves to support and enhance the dome. The wide flight of steps rising from the landing stage does not give a sense of direction, but forms a pedestal.

Guarini

Fate, which made Guarini an architect of Piedmont, also decreed that his longitudinal churches should be destroyed, and that only two of his centralized churches should survive. In the Cappella della SS Sindone, he has inscribed Borromini's triangle in the banal circle bequeathed to him by his predecessor. But instead of erasing the circle, he combined the two forms, so that three strange segments of lifeless space adhere to the sides of the triangle. As the eye rises from the gloom at floor level towards the luminous lantern, it follows the conflict of circular forms and ternary rhythms. Three tympana rest on the cornice, but like the pendentives which separate them, they are pierced by circular windows which recall the claims of the rival scheme. The dome supported on these tympana rises from a circular base, but the small alternating pediments which are woven, as it were, into the inner surface, form a stack of triangular cells which decrease in size the nearer they get to the ring of the lantern.

S Lorenzo is even further removed from Borromini, the optical effects interfering with the geometric variations. The ground plan of the nave is a kind of square, which becomes an octagon at the level of the entablature, only to become a Greek cross by the time it reaches the pendentives. The base of the dome is circular, that of the lantern again octagonal. The dome is supported by eight ribs forming a lattice similar to those found in certain mosques and Romanesque churches in Spain. To this superposition of contradictory central plans is added an elliptical choir, as at the Salute. The high altar, separated from the nave by a convex and a concave archway, receives light from a hidden dome – devices drawn from Bernini.

The Austrian central plan

The intrusion of Roman Baroque into the religious architecture of Central Europe coincided largely with that of the central plan. It is by virtue of its plan and its resulting austere dignity that the Church of the Knights Templar at Prague stands out from the other churches built there in the first sixty years of the century. Salzburg at its peak refused to have any other form. In the Trinity, Fischer von Erlach contented himself with restoring the longitudinal axis to the oval which Bernini had set crosswise in S Andrea. Confirming his loyalty to Rome, he deployed a wide concave façade with strongly accentuated wings, to either side of entrance, leaving the dome to stand free in the center. This icy reminder of S Agnese heralded Neo-Classicism right across the eighteenth century by means of its two pairs of inert, coupled columns. It seemed as though this twofold lesson from Bernini and Borromini might endanger mere academism north of the Alps.

Fischer himself gave the lie to this in two opposing styles. At the University Church in Salzburg he supported a domed Greek-cross central plan with four minor chapels roofed with cupolas. His difficulty lay in how to attach these chapels to the nave without losing their autonomy or clumping them together in a side-aisle. He extended them upwards in defiance of all proportion. They pierce narrow openings in the floors of the galleries, rising to roof level, and extend beyond it in tubular lanterns. They draw the eye upwards through the various levels like a telescope, and it is this long vertical perspective which keeps them separate. Between these four chimney-like chapels, as vertiginous as Le Corbusier's Ronchamp, the central space rises between its eight white perpendicular cliffs; their monumental upsurge is stressed and echoed by the columns of the choir, which rise free like obelisks.

In the Karlskirche, on the other hand, Fischer restores priority to the longitudinal axis. There is a return to the oval of the Trinity at Salzburg, brought alive by a magnificent choir. As Fischer had integrated Borromini's curves with the two-towered façade so dear to Central Europe in his strikingly original University Church, so in the Karlskirche and the Trinity he revived the wide front and flanking wings of S Agnese. This time, however, the transposition was masterly. The two towers, reduced to the state of squat pagodas, bear massively down, closing the façade to right and left, but yield to the two Trojan columns the role of framing the dome and

speeding its upward curve, entrusted by Borromini to his two towers at S Agnese. The delicacy of the portico accentuates the immensity of the dome, giving it complete dominance. The balance established by the Roman architect here becomes a matter of hierarchy. In place of the powerful unity of the threefold composition of the Piazza Navona is a multiple plurality, whose functions are distinctly divided yet miraculously dominated by a fleeting, undisputable vision of the imperial ideal.

Kiritein (Moravia): Pilgrim Church, by Ritz

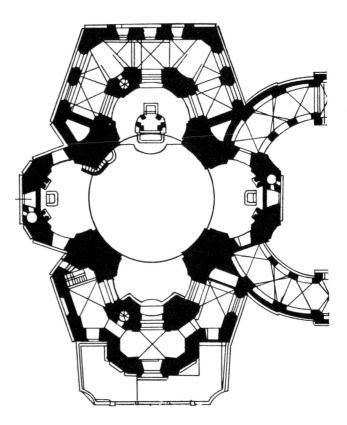

The special forms of the central and longitudinal plans in Moravia, Switzerland and Germany

The heritage of the Seicento was not restricted to a single formula, for Guarini also taught the Prague architects how to alter the essence of the oblong plan. In his Church of S Maria-della-Divina-Providenza at Lisbon, Guarini designed an undulating line of galleries and, in S Filippo at Turin, triangular piers whose apexes pierce the nave, whose unity is thus continually in question. These two innovations radically altered the interior of St Nicholas in Mala Strana, making its prototype, the Gesù, seem very dated. At the Benedictine monastery of Raigern in Moravia, Aichel constructed in succession a longitudinal oval, an octagon and then a transverse oval, thus realizing a composite area with a clear orientation – a highly personal and spectacular adaptation of an Italian design. The current of centralization can be felt in the crossing of St Nicholas, and is barely held in check in the half-way octagon at Raigern. It appears, however, that at the beginning of the eighteenth century, the central plan tended to be used for special purposes, being to a certain extent associated with the program of pilgrim churches. Aichel's work confirms this assumption, particularly in the Greek crosses of Maria-Teinitz and Kiritein and the pentagon of St John Nepomuk on the Green Hill at Saar. A galleried ambulatory formed from five ellipses alternating with five curvilinear triangles surrounds the nave at Saar. This unusual rhythm evokes the five stars that shone over the Vltava when the Saint was thrown into the river. This is the most direct architectural monument to the patron saint of Bohemia who is inseparable from the Baroque landscapes of Central Europe.

Germany and Switzerland also seem to have this plan with a particular function, whereas in Rome it was viewed as the answer to a problem of aesthetics. In 1675, when Zuccalli planned a

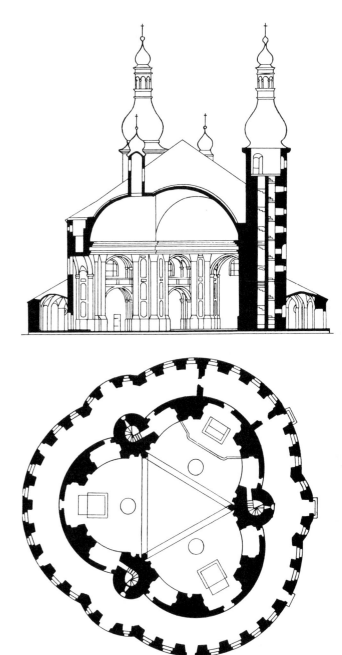

Holy Trinity Church, Käppel: section and plan, by Dientzenhofer (after Koepf)

101

church for the famous Bavarian shrine of Altötting, the clergy suggested that he make a large-scale reproduction of the old circular sanctuary in which the image of the Virgin was kept on view. At Käppel, near the Czech frontier, Georg Dientzenhofer combined local tradition with the themes of Borromini when he drew up his plans of three semi-circles linked to the sides of a central triangle. The allusion is quite explicit; the pilgrims of Käppel were honoring the Trinity. In S Ivo, two of the apses are empty; each of Dientzenhofer's three apses, on the other hand, contain one main and two secondary altars. Three similar towers stand out from the body of the church, irrefutably proclaiming the basic dogma.

It has been said that the wide naves of the central plan churches made it easier to accommodate crowds of pilgrims, while the surrounding galleries facilitated their movement. These purely functional considerations did not, however, justify every plan. It seems to be established beyond doubt that the central plan was well-suited to the modest dimensions of the pilgrim church, endowing it with a rarified, precious atmosphere which helped to direct the somewhat dumbfounded admiration of the faithful towards the reliquaries. It contrived to make the church into a sort of curiosity whose fame spread far and wide, and this contributed as much to the pilgrims' desire to journey to the shrine as did the reputation of the wonder-working statue or the miraculous picture.

The majority of ordinary parish churches and those which served a neighboring monastery, remained longitudinal in plan. They were no

St Urban: Pilgrim Church, by Franz Beer and Peter Thumb (after Koepf)

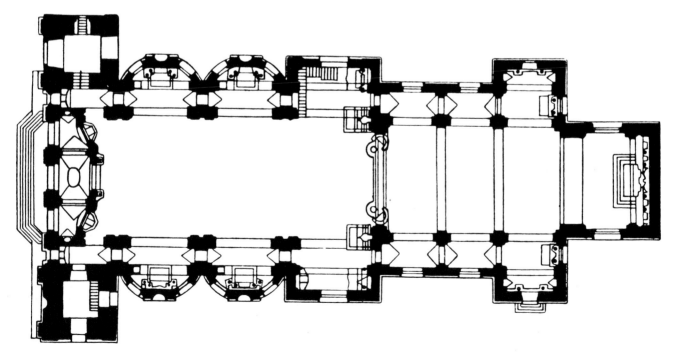

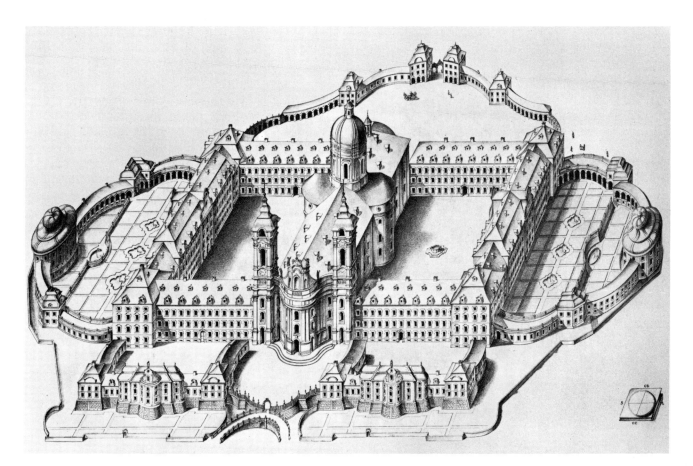

Weingarten Convent: overall view
(after a contemporary engraving)

longer the routine imitations of medieval models, however, nor were they mechanical repetitions of sixteenth-century Italian types, unquestioningly following the post-Tridentine rules. The architects of Vorarlberg gave new life to the traditional right-angled scheme, turning it into a simple, adaptable plan which was admittedly similar to that of the Gesù, but nevertheless animated by a very different spirit, and giving it firm roots in Southern Germany and Switzerland. The Vorarlberg church is angular and rather rough, its divisions are clearly defined, in particular the bays of the nave. To the right and left of each bay are two corresponding chapels, framed and isolated by wall pillars, short sections of wall perpendicular to the outside wall, forming buttresses. The transept is usually insignificant, consisting of one bay a little longer and wider than the others. The side chapels are as high as the nave, but are divided by a gallery which powerfully emphasizes the rhythmic movement of the church towards the East by means of its horizontal line. The scheme was put to use in the mid-seventeenth century in the period of the High Baroque. In addition to Obermachtel, the Thumb family's most noted works before 1700 were Schönenberg and Friedrichshafen; Franz Beer had designed Holzen and Irrsee. A few years later, he produced some variations at Rheinau near Schaffhausen and at St Urban in the Canton of Solothurn. He pierced doors in the wall pillars, in particular, which resulted in the creation of a rough form of side aisle. There is a similar innovation at Disentis in the Grisons and at Weingarten in Swabia, dating from about 1715. It seems likely that the architect responsible here was Gaspard Moosbrugger, the brilliant representative of an intermediate generation of the Vorarlberg school that formed a link between Michael Thumb of Obermachtel and Peter Thumb of St Gallen. At Weingarten, however, the problem is complicated by the presence of Frisoni, an architect from Como. With its dome at the crossing, its transepts with their rounded ends, and its sober, dignified lines, this church constitutes a unique example of the combination of the rustic plan and the Italianate nobility of the cathedral at Salzburg.

The combination of the central plan and the oblong plan in the pilgrim churches

At his own monastery at Einsiedeln, Moosbrugger was faced by a new problem; the church had to serve simultaneously as a pilgrim church and as an abbey. His solution was perfectly logical; a central octagonal space was linked to the end of a right-angled church. More logically still, the Virgin and Child, the object of the pilgrimage, occupies the center of the octagon; the chapel which shelters it is backed by two pillars which are linked to the periphery by eight ribs. Although it is solidly bound to the main structures, the crowd can move round it without disrupting the kneeling worshipers. There is a smooth transition from here to the oblong part of the church: the bay which adjoins the octagon is a large one, covered by a very flattened dome on a square base. It is only after this transition

near the entrance to the choir, that the visitor becomes fully aware of the movement of the longitudinal axis.

But the combination of the two systems did not always result from a duality of function. Although Steinhausen and Wies are purely pilgrim churches, Zimmermann did not merely give them the central plan. He subordinated their oval naves to the magnetic movement of a choir, after the fashion of Bernini and Fischer von Erlach. In actual fact, the role of the central spaces in these churches differs entirely from the octagon of Einsiedeln, for they contain no holy image. The pilgrims gathered together in them after their long journey to give thanks after the worship. Their curved sides emanate a warm welcome and peace regained. The pillars, single or in pairs, seem to form a sort of ambulatory round the nave, though in actual fact the distance separating them from the outside wall is minimal, it is difficult to move round this so-called gallery, especially at Wies, and processions are out of the question. The colonnades are an essential contribution to the stability of the assembly area, stressing its relative independence from the rest of the building.

The east ends of these churches frame the high altar, where the holy statue is enshrined, and heighten its effect. Here the sense of movement reigns supreme and one feels impelled to draw as close as possible to the Pietà of Steinhausen and the Flagellation of Wies. The choir galleries direct the glance with their horizontal line which cuts the walls at about a third of their full height. But not only do they indicate the path the eyes must take; because of them the pilgrim can avoid the choir itself and almost touch the high altar.

The conflict between the longitudinal axis and the central plan tradition in German pilgrim churches is part of the history of Vierzehnheiligen. Neumann and the Bishop of Bamberg, Friedrich-Karl von Schönborn, were set on a basilica, and the Abbot of Langheim had commissioned a Saxon architect to design a rotunda. The rotunda was scornfully rejected by the Schönborn faction, but the Saxon remained at the head of building operations and distorted Neumann's original plan sufficiently to force him to make a compromise. The idea of a basilica dominates the exterior, giving it a purely classical look; German Baroque, moreover, took no interest in façades, and in the case of the silhouette, its only important innovation was the elimination of the dome from the crossing. In the interior, however, the pilgrim church plan triumphs. Though the original Latin-cross plan remains discernible, Neumann has neutralized the basic articulations. The choir is atrophied and the crossing literally no longer exists. The point where the dome should have been and where Fischer and the Vorarlberg architects erected a wide flattened vault which still retains a character of its own, coincides at Vierzehnheiligen with the meeting of four vaults. The junction of two perpendicular areas no longer dominates the building; it merely represents one episode in a spatial adventure full of surprises and apparent contradictions. At the other end of the church, near the entrance, a half-sketched transept first disrupts the orientation. In this way the commemorative altar, placed paradoxically in the middle of the nave, becomes the pivot of this fake basilica. The great arcades of the center bay curve inwards into their galleries, forming an ellipse round it. The worshipers of the fourteen Saints are immediately drawn towards it and the area spreads out again from it as if in concentric circles. This is a far cry from the work of Moosbrugger and Zimmermann; the complexity

Frauenkirche, Dresden: section and plan, by Bähr (after Koepf)

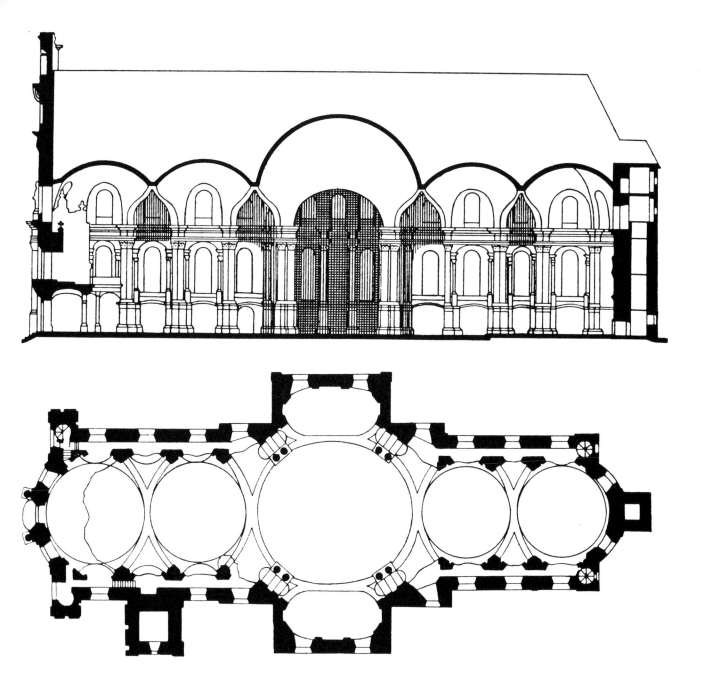

Convent Church at Neresheim: section and plan,
by Neumann (after Koepf)

is not the result of any addition. It is as if the pilgrim element had forced its way into a traditional structure and disrupted it.

Unintentional combinations of the central and oblong plans

One must hastily add, however, that the nostalgia for rotundas was not a characteristic exclusive to the architects of pilgrim churches. Protestant architects with their ideas for a hall with uninterrupted vision, were led to centralize some of their churches, including the Frauenkirche at Dresden, into the form of auditoria. At the crossing of Ottobeuren the visitor is conscious of a perceptible slowing of the rhythm, a majestic pause, alien to the customary progression of South German churches; violent bursts of light from the sides break onto the inexorable procession of wall pillars. At Rott-am-Inn, J. M. Fischer consciously and almost gratuitously pursues the integration of a circle and a rectangle. The perfect symmetry of his church round its two axes and the structure of its central space are both new. Into a central plan Fischer introduces four chapels framed by wall pillars, such as are usually to be found bordering longitudinal naves. The conflict of the two main axes is thus forgotten.

However, experiments continued, giving an air of family likeness to the last three great churches of the Benedictines, Neresheim, St Gallen and Wiblingen. The half-way rotunda seems to become as inevitable as a cathedral transept. At Neresheim it is combined with two transepts, and in certain plans for St Gallen, drawn up by Johann-Michael Beer, the predecessor of Peter Thumb, the idea of a circular enlargement is seen, significantly, in conflict with that of a transverse rectangle.

The originality of Neresheim, Neumann's last work, which was largely completed after his death, does not lie in the insertion of wide, calm

ellipse between a nave and choir also formed from elliptical bays with a clear orientation, but rather in the harmonies existing between these elements with their two traditional contradictions. The flat dome at the crossing seems to rest on its own supports, four pairs of tall columns, standing free of the walls which envelop the church with their geometrical angles. This slender framework remains detached up to the level of the entablature. Junction with the walls is effected at the level of the vaults by means of the sinuous arches already used by Neumann at Vierzehnheiligen; these rise obliquely, stretching out one to another, and merging halfway along their span. The rectilinear walls of the nave and choir are the product of a fusion; Neumann was again haunted, as his plans show, by the idea of a basilica made up of three naves. He wished, despite everything, to enlarge and free his main nave, and gradually drew back the great arcades with their galleries towards the outside walls, producing a double wall, or rather one very thick wall pierced by three longitudinal galleries one above the other. This magnificent 'wall' strongly articulated like a Roman wall, with its disturbed contrasts reminiscent of a late façade by

Convent Church at Wiblingen, by Georg Specht. The façade is allied to that of Einsiedeln (after Koepf)

Borromini, is one of the masterpieces of late Baroque.

At St Gallen, the Vorarlberg church has lost its wall pillars, or rather they have been reduced to isolated columns, whose sequence transforms the church into a basilica. At the third pillar, the aisles curve inwards, three of their bays forming the edge of the middle rotunda. This is the least mysterious of the central areas we have discussed, and it springs not from the intersection of four axes as at Rott-am-Inn nor from the insertion of a special structure at a key point as at Neresheim, but from the simple distortion of the normal plan, a practical rather than a geometrical solution. Peter Thumb, who had abandoned the usual family scheme at Birnau, took it up again at St Gallen to demonstrate its almost inexhaustible potential. From the archtype of longitudinal churches he extracted the most striking effect of width to be found in this period.

A different spirit reigns over the huge white hall of Wiblingen, which dates from some fifteen years later. The nave is built on a square plan, and is not opposed by the rotunda, but almost repeats it. The choir, also nearly a square, lacks the force to create a sense of orientation. The three sections of the church are not linked by a single movement but simply by similarity. The unity of the interior does not change according to one's position, but exerts the same clear, static influence from every viewpoint.

Ten years later, a single step is sufficient to end the Baroque era at St Blasien. In 1783, Michael d' Ixnard, who had made his first hesitating attempts to create a style of his own at Buchau, here made a radical breakthrough by setting down the Pantheon of Agrippa in the middle of the Black Forest. The vast domed cylinder of St Blasien, in its isolation and self-sufficiency, sheds a retrospective light on the direction taken by the researches of Fischer von Erlach, J. M. Fischer and Neumann. The choir, an over long and narrow appendage which was added later, looks out of place and exerts no domination over the central space. The church is divided into two quite distinct sections which are irreconcilable; one is for the use of the monks, the other is for ceremonial occasions, but was too large for eighteenth-century worshipers and has the same effect on present-day tourists. One style of architecture is dead, and with it died architecture as a whole for more than a century, since the places used in prayer and the leading of life from day to day are no longer those dedicated to the display of beauty.

The efforts of the Italians of the Seicento and later of the masters of the Rococo, to perpetuate the steady advance of Western Christianity through the closed forms of Antiquity and Byzantium, seem sometimes to have been gratuitous exercises in literary attitudes. The pompous failure of St Blasien, on the contrary, reveals what they meant to architecture over a span of one hundred and fifty years – a rejection of the facile, the humdrum, the desire to subject oneself to a creative discipline, a hatred of pastiche. About 1920, a group of great architects tried to adapt their work to the needs of mankind, revealing the presence of simple geometrical forms and giving them a sort of a priori common denominator. The aims of the Baroque architects were not far removed from these. They strove to facilitate the act of worship, to reunite the faithful beneath the pulpit, before the altar and to make every church the projection of a sacred order of things. From this standpoint, the ellipses of Bernini and Neumann and the triangles of Borromini are equivalent to the cuboid forms of Gropius, Le Corbusier and Mies van der Rohe.

Plates

Obermachtel

113 **The Abbey Church.** North bays of nave and choir. Church of Vorarlberg type, with heavy wall pillars, pierced at gallery level, but solid below, a straight line of galleries, one deeper bay resembling the arm of a transept.

114 The vault at the entrance to the choir. High Baroque stucco work, all in white, fairly thick, evoking rather stylized plant forms.

115 The high altar. Fine example of High Baroque retable in brown gilded wood, balanced and articulated. Twisted columns. The retable placed against the wall pillar at the entrance to the choir (see plate 113) is in the same style.

116 Three bays on the south side of the choir. The capitals with their huge angular abacus design weigh down the pillars, testifying to the stability of the church.

Banz

117 **The Abbey.** The monastery buildings from the north east (the side facing the Main valley).

118 Façade on to the court of honor and great staircase.

119 Façade of the church.

120 The nave. The walls have almost entirely disappeared; they are only represented by the two concave sections facing each other in the middle of the nave. The pilasters are set at an angle, as in St Nicholas in Mala Strana; here the oblique arches which surmount them remain visible. Note the two retables set obliquely at the entrance to the choir, directing the eye towards the high altar. The picture which seems to form its center is actually situated some thirty meters beyond the portico. Predominating colors are brown, white and gold.

121 The galleries and vaults, very typical of the Dientzenhofer style. The undulating galleries evoke those of St Nicholas in Mala Strana. The arches unite at the head of the vault, defining on one side a wide, more or less oval vault covered by a large fresco, and on the other, small triangular vaults, hollowed out by 'penetrations' above the galleries.

Munich

122 **St John Nepomuk.** The nave, seen through the grille of the narthex.

123 The nave at first floor level, and the vault, viewed from below. The Trinity is depicted above the choir, at cornice level: the Father, seated and wearing a tiara, is helped by angels to hold a silver crucifix suspended in mid-air. Above him, the Dove of the Holy Ghost hovers amid a 'Glory' supported in turn on the wings of four angels set on four twisted columns. This group occupies the most important position in the whole church.

124 Heads of cherubs.

Steinhausen

125 **Pilgrim Church.** The end of the nave with the organ gallery.

126 The nave from the organ gallery. In the foreground, the gilded wooden balustrade. In the background, the high altar, on the upper level of which is the Pietà. On either side of the two altars, set slantwise right and left of the entrance to the choir, are sections of the balustrade common to pilgrim churches: these direct the pilgrims along the choir walls to the level of the sacred image. Access to them is by doors opening into the outer gallery behind the obliquely set altars. The columns of the nave describe an ellipse whose main axis leads to the choir entrance. The vault fresco, partly visible, depicts earthly paradise. The dominant colors are white and pink with touches of green and gold.

127 Right-hand side of the nave from the choir. The shape of the windows on the right is typical of Zimmermann.

128 Detail of the capitals.

The Abbey, Banz, by Dientzenhofer
Plan 1:400

The Abbey Church, Obermachtel, by Thumb
Plan of the cloister with position of the Abbey Church 1:1000

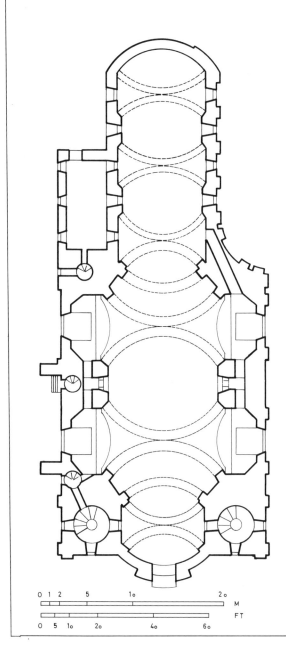

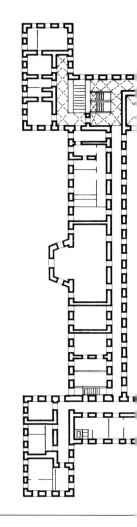

```
0 1 2    5       1o              2o
                                        M
                                        FT
0  5  1o      2o         4o         6o
```

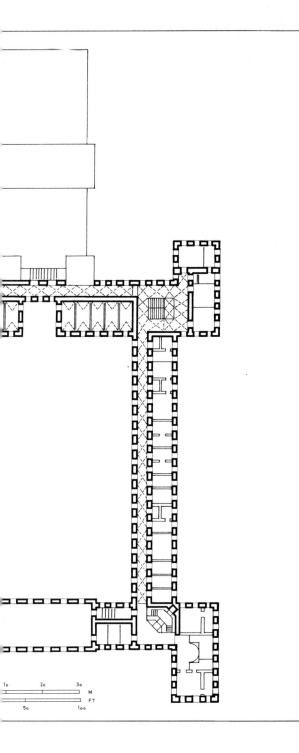

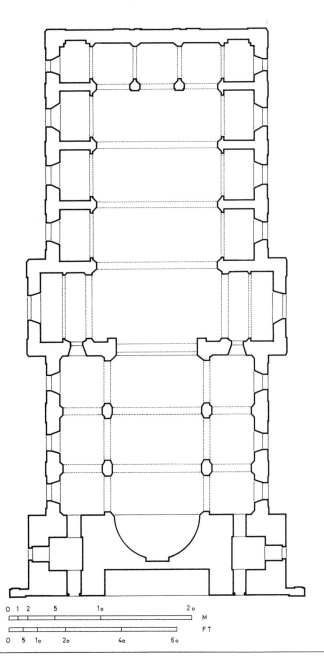

Plan of the Abbey Church 1:400

Notes

Obermachtel

Abbey Church

On the road from Ulm to Sigmaringen, near Riedlingen, in Swabia. Imperial Abbey, that is to say, admitting no overlord other than the Emperor. Premonstratensian order. Built 1686-1692, under the direction of Michael Thumb and, subsequently, of his younger brother, Christian, and his cousin, Franz Beer. Modest dimensions: approximate length 168 feet; approximate width 66 feet (78 feet at the transept); approximate height 78 feet. Stuccos by J. Schmutzer of Wessobrunn. The High Baroque retables in the choir and transept are by the woodworker Speisegger and the sculptor Etschmann (1696-1698). Michael Thumb (1640-1690) was one of the earliest masters of the Vorarlberg guild. Chief works, besides Obermachtel, are the Jesuit college at Landshut (1667), the abbey church of Wettenhausen (1670), the Jesuit church at Ellwangen, the pilgrim church of Schönenberg (1682) and the church at Grafrath (1686).

Banz

The Abbey

Dominates the main valley opposite Vierzehnheiligen, three kilometers from Staffelstein. Benedictines attached to the reformed Cluniac Order by Hirsau in 1114. Most of the monastery buildings by Leonhard Dientzenhofer date from the early years of the eighteenth century. The court of honor and the exterior portico for which Neumann provided designs in 1750, were executed by Küchel and completed in 1772. The church is by Leonhard's younger brother, Johann, and was built between 1710 and 1719. Small dimensions: the nave, without the chapels, measures less than 90 feet by 39 feet. The frescoes are the work of the Tyrolean painter, Melchior Steidl, and those on the three nave vaults have a thematic progression: the first represents the conversion of St Paul, the second the Holy Ghost and the third, the Last Supper. Leonhard Dientzenhofer (1640-1707) held the post of official architect to the Bishop of Bamberg and built parts of the abbey of Ebrach and the Bamberg Residenz. Johann (1663-1726) succeeded him, having erected the abbey church of Fulda in the early years of the century, after a journey to Italy.

He is known to have collaborated in the building of Pommersfelden with his master, Elector Lothar Franz.

Munich

St John Nepomuk

The private foundation of Egid-Quirin Asam who, between 1729 and 1733, bought four houses in the Sendlingergasse for this purpose. One was for the priest, another for the architect himself, and the church occupied the site of the other two. Foundation stone laid in 1733 on the feast day of SS Cosmas and Damian. The façade went up in 1735 and the church was consecrated in 1746. Stuccos by Egid-Quirin; fresco by Cosmas Damian; tabernacle by Ignaz Günther. Approximate length 84 feet; width 27 feet. The church was linked directly to Egid-Quirin's house. The choir and the ceiling fresco were damaged in 1944 and again in 1945. Restoration was completed in 1948. The windows in the upper part of the choir which were blocked up by a large picture in the nineteenth century, have been restored to their original form. C. D. Asam (1686-1739) and Egid-Quirin Asam (1692-1750) were sons of the painter Hans-Georg Asam. In 1711 they were sent to Rome by the abbot of Tegernsee. Their buildings include Weltenburg (1716), Rohr (1717) St John Nepomuk and the Church of the Ursulines at Straubing (1736). They did the decoration at Weingarten, St Jakobi at Innsbruck, Aldersbach, Freising Cathedral, St Emmeram at Regensburg, Brevnov and Kladran, Einsiedeln, Osterhofen, Fürstenfeldbruck and St Maria Victoria at Ingolstadt.

Steinhausen

Pilgrim Church

In a village of 300 inhabitants near Biberach in Swabia. Built by Dominikus Zimmermann for the Imperial Abbey of the Premonstratensians at Schussenried, 1728-1735. One of the most staggering examples of over-expenditure in the whole history of architecture: though the contract was for 9,000 guilders, 40,000 were in fact spent, and as a result, the abbot was forced to retire. Dominikus Zimmermann also executed the stuccos; the frescoes are by his brother, Johann Baptist, and the altars by Joachim Früholzer, a sculptor from Weingarten. Approximate length 105 feet, width 63 feet. Zimmermann was born at Wessobrunn in 1685 and died in 1766. After Steinhausen, he built Günzburg (1736) and Wies (1745).

St John Nepomuk, Munich, by Asam
Plan 1:200

Pilgrim Church, Steinhausen, by Zimmermann
Plan 1:300

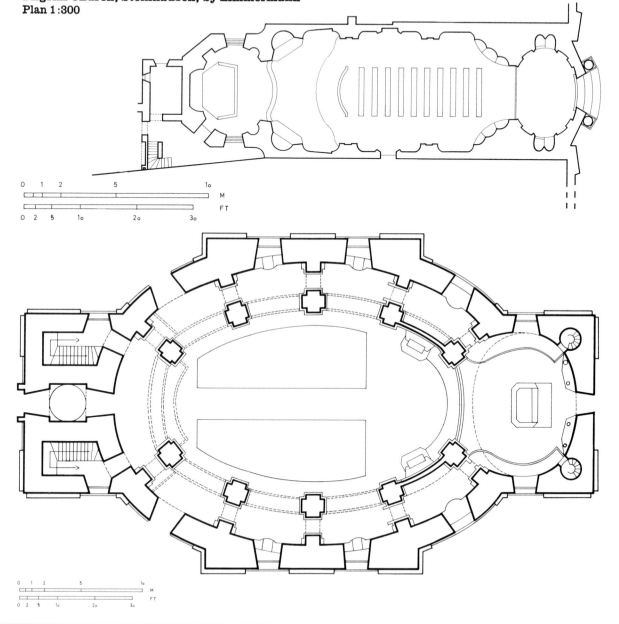

129

The Abbey Church, Zwiefalten, by Fischer
Elevation (after Koepf) 1:600; plan 1:600

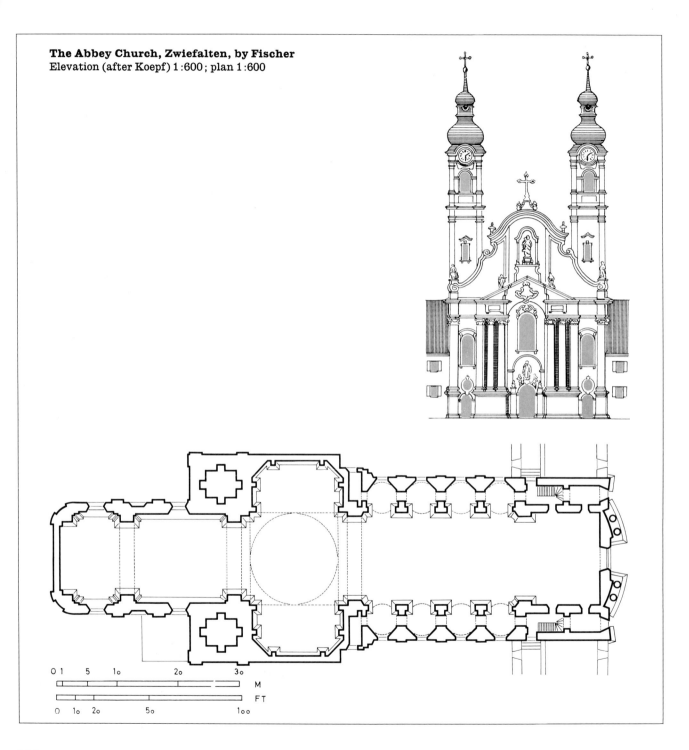

O 1   5   1o   2o   3o

M

FT

O   1o 2o   5o   1oo

3. Church Architecture: Enclosed Space and Technical Problems

Given the right proportions, the basic four walls and a vaulted roof or dome, we are faced as the case may be, by a finished Romanesque or Renaissance church. That element which brings the Baroque into being is still absent. The three-dimensional space enclosed within its walls of stone must await this catalyst before a Baroque church can be born. But this catalyst is an elusive ingredient, as one can gather from the different ways found to express it, 'a fourth dimension in architecture,' 'an organic proliferation of a teutonic form,' 'a centrifugal movement' and 'a supernatural ventilation' of enclosed space. However one seeks to define it, no spectator of the Baroque can ignore its presence from the moment he steps over the threshold of the building – nor can he foresee its potential beforehand.

Viewed as an architectural ground plan, a large square room with an entrance on one of its sides does not appear very different from a similar room in which the door is placed obliquely across one of the corners. But any visitor passing successively through two such rooms will confirm without hesitation that his two experiences of enclosed space were radically opposed to one another. In the previous chapter we noticed that a Baroque ground-plan does not necessarily hamper the development of the structure built upon it, into something with its own traditions and fantasies. We will now show that the enclosed space of a Baroque building is in exactly the same way, and to the same extent, free from rigid laws. Enclosed space cannot be reduced to any sort of architectural diagram.

Cortona, Borromini, Rainaldi, Guarini and the destruction of the wall as a rigid factor in architecture

From the onset, Urban VIII's architects acted as if the undeniably functional role of enclosing walls were a kind of profanation of the very principles of religious architecture. Well aware of the fact that Brunelleschi's interiors or Alberti's façades had appealed above all to the rationalist spirit of Renaissance times, they were moved, it would seem, to do away with the suspect notions of inner and outer clarity of form, to do away, therefore, with the kind of wall which defined this form. The process did not prove to be as hazardous as might logically be presumed.

The history of architecture abounds in experiments to lessen the oppressive domination of the wall. Lombard architects and artists of the sixteenth century discovered a new weapon against the almost oppressively enclosing walls of the earlier Renaissance – this was the fresco. Such purely pictorial means were soon to be exploited by Baroque artists. In the meantime, the architectural generation of Bernini, Borromini, Carlo Rainaldi and even Pietra da Cortona found a precursor of genius who was nearer to their own taste.

In 1520, Michelangelo's sculptural treatment of the columns in the Biblioteca Laurenziana vestibule had already created a play of perspectives which gave an equivocal significance to the walls themselves. Roman architects drew upon the artistic consequences of this for the remainder of the century, thus preparing the way for the generation of 1630. At this point we must once more raise the question of so-called 'logical outcomes.' Was Baroque simply a logical and necessary sequel to Humanism – that is, Renaissance plus Religion? To answer this, we must first examine the functions assigned to the column during these two afore-mentioned periods.

A basic element of structure in trabeated architecture, the column had been endowed by the Greeks not only with a rigorously inflexible function, but also an imminent relationship with man himself – a sense of scale and measure above all of human perfection attainable on earth. The High Renaissance moved beyond man as a measure of scale (for example, the introduction of a giant order at St Peter's) but retained the geometrical purity of the classical principle of the function of the column: it must clarify the essence of a structure, just as it supports and decorates it. With the advent of the Baroque, this clarity vanishes. An element of disorder (the very term seems paradoxical in this context) appears.

A study of the column in relation to the 'space' surrounding it thus eliminates the distorting concept of it as a mere part of a structure. To see an echo of Renaissance experimentation in the design of the churches of SS Luca-e-Martina in Rome is only justifiable in so far as Cortona, like Leonardo da Vinci or Filarete, was moved by a certain ideal of a symmetrical, enclosing shell with a central focal point. Spatial truth once again – as in the analogy of the square rooms – is far removed from the conceptual fiction of the text books. Where indeed are the heavily outlined ground traits of Leonardo's sketches when one actually finds oneself within Cortona's building? Here the limits, the walls are in tangible, almost unperceptible. The columns stand in the nave yet, at the same time, they border it. What the eye perceives through the line of columns as receding space amounts, in fact, to no more than a pilaster's width; it is the wall, now apparently a void, which takes on the function of a mere accessory to structure. Liberated from its role of barrier, the wall becomes part of a discreet play of light and shade in exactly the same way as do the shafts of the columns, the entablatures and empty niches. It gives the enclosed space its essential quality – transforming a geometric volume into a living cell.

The Roman Baroque's battle against the tyranny of the wall took many forms. In

Borromini's S Carlo-alle-Quattro-Fontane the colonnades do not so much supplant the nave walls as stand out clear against them. In Rainaldi's S Maria-in-Campitelli, on the other hand, the columns accomplish what the walls of this heterogeneous building were incapable of doing on their own – the fusing of different sections of a composite interior. The ground-plan, one may recall, juxtaposes a Greek cross and a square hall – both traditional designs, considered separately, but requiring a touch of genius to blend them satisfactorily in a three-dimensional whole. The solution adopted here is one of complex rhythmic variations on a theme – the column. The combined effect boldly accen-tuates – and thereby justifies – the different 'phrases' of the whole – the varying patterns of columns which connect the parts of the building as one advances from the nave to the sanctuary.

Like Borromini, Cortona and Rainaldi in Rome, Guarini continued in Turin the process of reduc-tion of the wall to a border, capable of diffusing the interior with the kind of lighting that gave rise to effects of mirage. The final act of nega-tion of the wall can be seen in the arches of the nave in his Church of S Lorenzo. These convex porticoes erected in front of the walls and the angles of the nave challenge the structure itself. The columns attain complete independence.

Bernini and the construction of interior space

If we have insisted so far upon an essentially destructive tendency visible in Roman Baroque, our purpose will now become clear. The negation of any single vital architectural concept – in this case the wall seen as a form-limiting, en-closing shell – can only lead to the constructive exploitation of another one. If in reality two such phases co-exist and are even to be seen in the same structures, it is nevertheless true that what one has named 'exuberant Baroque' was first and foremost a movement of reaction, intent on demonstrating perfectly valid traditions. It now remains to describe the new, positive phenomenon over which the generation of 1630 triumphantly took its stand. The task is not easy – definitions, as we have seen, are out of the question. We are faced by a type of structure unique in architectural history.

Bernini was the first and undisputed master of the problem. Aware of the disruptive element inherent in the new ground-plans, he found an effective solution – an interior space free of specific structural definitions, but built up from the dynamic fusion of architectural, sculptural and pictorial elements. Bernini's discoveries made the rational limits of column, and the traditional barriers separating the three major constructional arts a thing of the past. Where formerly one could distinguish a hierarchy, in which painting and sculpture were subordinated to architecture, there now emerges a kind of fusion, with the building but the external mani-festation of sculptured and pictorial space. What was subordination has become equality. Baroque was, for the artist, synonymous with liberty.

Standing in the nave of S Andrea-del-Quirinale, the spectator senses something which escapes definition, most of all in archi-tectural terms. Light and color are so modulated that the space, in which the eye is drawn irresistibly upwards, seems shaped out of the different tones and textures present in the three levels of supporting vaulted structures. Three hundred years before Le Corbusier's time, 'canons of light' descend from above to be focused on the altar, while the eye moves up-wards, drawn by the polychromatic gradation from the reds of the lower portion to the clearer tones and pure white of the angels on the upper portion, finally attaining the white and gilt dome which forms a world of its own. It is his handling of this typical element of the Baroque – the dome – that reminds us of Bernini's talent as a sculptor. Figures heighten the effect of the dome. The scale of the different groups varies according to their position. This calculated disproportion – the figures on the lantern base too diminutive, those on the cornice too large – accentuate the feeling of soaring ascent, just as the perspective columns in Bernini's Scala Regia provoke an impression of space receding on an inclined plane. A second illusion is more spiritual than optical. The angels, so human in appearance close to us, are gradually transmuted into ethereal bodies, defying all laws of gravity as they soar upwards to the lantern. Just above the metaphorical flurry of angels' wings at the very crown of the dome, the Holy Dove announces the proximity of the divine.

None of these lessons was lost on the Baroque generations to come. The most fruitful legacy of all was, nevertheless, Bernini's twofold solution to the somewhat overpowering logic of the space beneath the dome of St Peter. The canopy came first, then thirty years later, the throne. The impact of these two structures on the history of architecture was decisive and without precedent: at the central crossing of the Basilica, itself erected at the heart of Christendom, was born an artistic fusion of architecture, sculpture and painting which transcended every conceivable past model produced by any one of these elements.

The very presence of the Baldacchino (Canopy) in St Peter's can be taken as a vigorous defiance of the surrounding structure which, despite Michelangelo's dome, was deemed insufficient on its own. The Renaissance had lavished its attention on the effecting of transitions between one surface and another, but in vain. The so-called 'finished envelope' had had to await the advent of Bernini before one realized that space itself required constructing. The Canopy was no freak of the imagination, it had and still has the rigor of a proof, even if the execution does not correspond to the underlying theory. The prestige lay in the attempt itself; the result was a challenging new principle, one soon to be heard north of the Alps, where, it seems, it was most needed. The Baroque of Northern Europe gave monumental value to what had been mere decoration elsewhere, thus effectively obliterating banal or over-fussy ground-plans.

The interior of Banz

Johann Dientzenhofer attempted at Fulda to repeat Bernini's experiments in St Peter's, and he also met with only partial success. The heavy basilican plan is not noticeably transformed by the Baldacchino, which is here provided with six columns and, enlarged into a slender triumphal arch, blocks the choir entrance without concealing the altar in the apse. At Banz, on the other hand, the effect is wholly successful. The arch terminating the nave and the large picture forty yards away at the back of the apse together form a huge double altarpiece which seizes the visitor like a trap. The choir has lost all impact, the visual role which its narrow, elongated form might have caused it to play being wholly transferred to an element of architectural decoration.

The church is not given its orientation by the choir, but by the retable of the high altar, with its two attendant altarpieces set slantwise at the eastern corners of the nave. When taken in conjunction with their opposite number in the western corners, these tend to make the nave into a central space. Dientzenhofer, having thus abolished his rectangular choir, brings the rectangle of his nave to life.

This is a twofold operation. First of all the central piers are modeled and the cornice and galleries designed according to the precepts of Guarini, with the result that the side walls can no longer be distinguished. The double direction of the arches of the vault with their converging curves abolishes the guiding line established by a vault divided into regular bays. At this point, mathematical Baroque has accomplished its destructive work and pictorial Baroque takes over with its decoys and illusions. In this sea of curves, chaotically disjointed walls and unrelated pilasters, beneath the undulating line of the vaults, the only points of rest are the four symmetrical, obliquely set altars, marking the outline of an imaginary oval.

It is a space whose contours are deceptive, but at the same time it gives an impression of life and warmth. Any attempt to work out the plan drives one to distraction; one must look for a logic at the very heart of this mass of shapes and colors. In short, it finds its own justification in its apparent confusion and lack of stability and its perpetual assault on our senses, because it gives us the sensation of something inexhaustible. The contribution of the altars to the spatial construction is twofold. In the first place, they act as landmarks or beacons, architectural posting-houses or moments of diversion. Secondly, they are the focus points of greatest tension in the swarming mass.

The Asam brothers' interior designs

With the Asam brothers, fervent pupils of Bernini, the altarpiece reigns supreme, although as a stage setting. At Osterhofen, Bernini's Baldacchino appears without basic modifications and the figures only play a subsidiary part. At Weltenburg and Rohr, however, the columns act as side scenery to conceal the wings. They do not frame the beginning or end of a perspective, but rather the spectacular re-living of a miracle, an emotive 'tableau-vivant' executed in stucco. For this reason, the interior of the church is arranged as an auditorium. The green and gold oval of Weltenburg is sacrificed to the manifestation of St George, and the long nave of Rohr, with its wall pillars, to the Assumption. In each case,

however, the 'production' is different. At Weltenburg the effects are thrown into violent relief. The intensity of feeling expressed is almost sufficient to throw the altarpiece out of balance. The altarpiece of Rohr, on the other hand, retains its monumental impassivity. Against the backcloth of a lightly folded, neutral-colored hanging, the Virgin and

Perspective study by Schübler

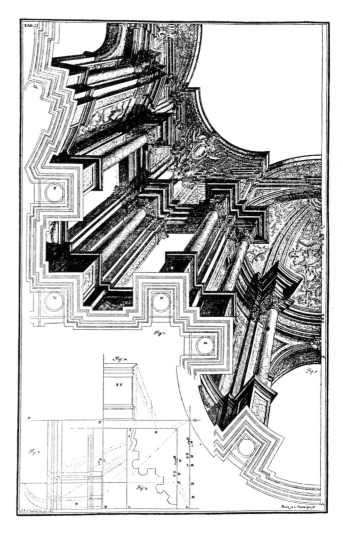

Apostles are bathed in ordinary mortal and equally distributed light. At Rohr, the eight men have approached the wonder as our representatives, but at Weltenburg the miracle overwhelms us.

The choirs in the early churches of the brothers Asam are theatrical; that of St John Nepomuk at Munich is the very essence of drama. The interior is no longer orientated so as to serve as a distant, captivating display; it is so ordered as to compel our participation. God is here and we are before Him. The ground level of the church is made entirely subservient to the upper storeys. The nave is narrow, the lower portions of the walls gray and bare. The encircling gallery is loaded with imitation red hangings and is linked to a sharply projecting entablature by the twisted columns that overhang the choir. In other words, the Baldacchino has been hoisted up to the first floor level. Instead of isolating the upper floor, the gallery becomes part of it, lending it vast weight. This results in a sense of an impending, overhanging threat. Right above the choir, however, at the base of the vault where there is a group of the three persons of the Trinity, rises a mysterious light. We instinctively raise our heads and follow the line of the beam. The interior acquires definition from this expressive diagonal.

Construction of the Rococo interior

To a certain extent the Rococo represents a return to abstraction. Spatial construction again becomes a metaphysical undertaking (as with Dientzenhofer) rather than an emotional one, though statuary does not lose its importance. There has been no architecture that made greater demands on sculpture than that movement in Würtemberg and Bavaria between 1730 and 1770. The emotion expressed by these saints and cherubs is, however, of less importance than their gestures and poses. They do not take part in a drama; they are part of the overall texture, emphasizing it and making it perceptible. Individually, they are of less importance than the invisible and lasting pattern of which they form the rich embroidery. This explains their movements, which cannot otherwise be accounted for either in psychological or symbolical terms and which have been compared to those of a dance.

Their gestures and accessories serve to exaggerate them. Ignaz Günther, the great mid-eighteenth century Bavarian sculptor, made a masterly use of croziers, crosses and scepters to open up the silhouettes of the altarpieces at Rott-am-Inn. At Rohr one of the awestruck apostles extends his arms wide, holding in his right hand a stick which makes his pose the more expressive; at the high altar of Rott, however, there is no justification for the angle formed by the cross of St Ulrich tilted to the right and his body to the left – apart from the desire to create two lines of vision. Günther integrates the figure with the altarpiece by means of the cross. On the other hand, it is linked with its surroundings by the miter which projects outwards following the thrust of the body. The statue with its companion, St Corbinien, and those of St Gregory and Cardinal Peter Damian in one of the side chapels, fulfils the function of a turntable, linking the altarpiece with the church as a whole.

By definition, the Glories which spread their rays from the summits of the altars are also pure divergences. Here the theme is all the more significant as it is systematically developed at the level where the image of God appears, and to which soar up the Assumptions and Adorations. The Glory clearly symbolizes a dazzling triumph; it is the instrument of Transfiguration. At the same time, however, it deprives God of his isolation, just as his prelates are deprived of theirs by means of their obliquely set insignia.

The God of Rococo altarpieces makes less

claim on our attention because He is almost always presented as the Trinity. The Three figures may be closely grouped as at Rott-am-Inn, or clearly spaced out in their hierarchy as at Fürstenfeld where the Son, bathed in earthly light, leans towards mankind, whilst the Father, half-glimpsed in the shadow of a canopy, appears to be seated on the boundary of two worlds. One is forced to look from one to the other, thus reuniting Them according to orthodox dogma. Moreover, the dialogue is renewed around the Father and Son.

With the aid of our imagination, the radiant Glories and the statues with their accentuated diagonals exceed all spatial limits, and the naves are filled with flying angels. The architects of the 1730's certainly did not invent these beings, but they were the first to free them from their earthly bonds and transform them into the living image of movement. The sculptor catches them in full flight, parallel to the ground, rising from it or descending head-first; he attaches them in the most precarious manner to the decoration; by a toe, a piece of creeper, or a cushion of cloud. The paraphernalia of the saints – cardinals' hats, liturgical objects and instruments of torture – lose all sense of weight, and escape the laws of gravity which create immovable rigid systems riveted to their central point. The heavy stucco hangings with their warm colors, the overloaded pulpits, thus lose their sense of massiveness and are swept away by this dynamic creative force.

In short, the Rococo is an art of imminent promise, a systematic exercise of possibilities. Thus it can be fundamentally identified in the shell and scroll work found everywhere on mid-eighteenth century altarpieces and pulpits, on the keystone of arches, especially those of the vault, on the cornerstones above the capitals and encircling the frescoes. These scrolls are completely asymmetrical, and defy geometrical analysis; their basic purpose is to make one feel the need for something more. They branch out into profuse tangles, but the branches which stem from them are inextricably confused. Everything is possible, but nothing is complete. We may chart this so-called 'progress' by a comparison with the stucco work of the High Baroque which had to swell and proliferate in order to banish the vacuum. In actual fact, however, it only served to thicken the walls and ceilings. In a way, it was no more than a repetition of the aim of Manneline architecture: the abundant, yet petrified forms of the churches of the 1680's, like Tomar and Belem, have no heirs and no future. They have more or less eliminated the void, but it continues to gape around and above them. The seething abundance of Banz is a wonderful success, but its density is oppressive. At St John Nepomuk this sense of oppression increases, yet is insignificant. The Rococo achieves plenitude by means of a device. There is no need to cover surfaces: a few twists and arabesques of scrollwork are all that is needed to completely obliterate them. It is enough to describe a few loops, thus outlining the surround.

The high altar and the orientation of the interior

Interior space must be uninterrupted but not unaccented. Its center must be detailed but not inextricable or devoid of issue. The swarming Rococo both helps the structure and interferes with it; sometimes it runs counter to the general orientation with its hesitating or sham verticals, but more often it makes it irresistible, transforming it violently.

In most churches the power of the high altar is made absolute through the medium of the altarpiece. There had been fine altarpieces in High Baroque churches like Obermachtel, but they were placed flat against the wall, seeming to paper the back of the choir and their dark woods and gilded statues did not modify its volume and mass. To a certain extent they resembled German fifteenth-century altarpieces, sumptuous pieces that seemed indissolubly linked to the masonry. Eighteenth-century altarpieces, on the other hand, were separated from the apse wall, thus acquiring a certain monumental independence, although they did not, like those of Dientzenhofer and E. Q. Asam, derive directly from Bernini's Baldacchino. Paradoxically enough, however, this caused them to become inseparable from the church.

When the Baroque conversion of ancient churches did not merely consist of applying an even layer of usually insipid plasterwork to the walls, it certainly implied the building of a retable for the high altar rising as high as the vault. This was not just hankering after excessive pomp, nor a futile desire to cast a veil over the so-called barbarian architecture of previous ages. It arose from the need to bring the high altar into scale with the church. In a Gothic cathedral it would be made to the scale of the choir. The Spanish architects went one step further, breaking the perspective of the nave with their sculptured choir screens, reducing the choir to the role of chapels. On the other hand, the huge altarpieces of Fischer and Zimmermann impose a fierce unity, acting as pedestals for an apotheosis which is re-echoed in the ceiling frescoes. They belong as much to the ordinary member of the congregation as to the most important worshiper. Because of their influence the whole church, however complicated its plan may be, acquires the intimacy and warmth of a chapel. Their final contribution is again ambiguous. While helping to establish an axis, lending magnetic power to the east end of the church, they simultaneously indicate how vain it is to approach that point. The pilgrim churches superbly justify this twofold aim; the great altarpieces of Steinhausen, Andechs and Wies stress the holy image. They also increase its range so that the pilgrims who are halted in the nave and cannot see it clearly, are yet aware of its proximity. When the church is half empty, the altarpiece acts as a pole of attraction so that each pilgrim can establish a personal relationship with Christ or the Virgin. When the nave is full its centrifugal power is still evident.

The role of secondary altarpieces

The Rococo's great discovery was the placing of the major altarpiece within a system of which it was, so to speak, the keystone. The High Baroque architects of Italy, Austria and Germany had increased the number of secondary altarpieces, but they were placed at the ends of side chapels or against aisle walls parallel to the longitudinal axis of the nave. Thus each one gave rise to division and rivalry, causing the worshiper to turn in his tracks, exacting individual prayers from him and holding back the devotees of minor saints. About 1730, the arrangement of the altars was changed, at any rate in churches of longitudinal plan, and they were placed against the wall pillars with their backs to the choir. Thus, as one enters the nave, it appears to be lined with a series of altarpieces at right angles to its axis, framed by the perspective leading up to the high altar. The design is now perfectly coherent. The high altar holds sway over the church not only by virtue of its brilliance and prominent proportions, but also on account of these preparatory sketches which herald it at intervals, increasing in richness and complexity as they approach the choir.

Coming back to the idea of the theater, the graduated scheme of wings and side-scenery for which Longhena provided a sketch at the Salute, and which characterizes the altarpieces of Rohr and Weltenburg, is applied to the Vorarlberg plan and now includes the whole interior. With the brothers Asam, in their early work at least, the stage was limited to the last bay of the choir. At Aldersbach, Fürstenfeld, Zwiefalten,

Structural designs: Italian School (Fatio Collection)

Diessen and even at Obermachtel where five Rococo altarpieces were added to the side chapels between 1727 and 1738, the stage embraces the entire church, and it is easy for us to make our entry. We do not, however, immediately come face to face with an explicit drama, as in St John Nepomuk at Munich. Surrounded by vague characters and fleeting motifs, we are gradually made aware of a vast murmuring fraught with allusion. Lost amid scenery too rich to be immediately interpreted, we feel ourselves imperceptibly drawn from bay to bay, from altarpiece to altarpiece.

There are other arrangements of altarpieces which are in no way influenced by the traditions of theatrical scenery, Torelli's flying colonnades or Pozzo's successions of porticoes. They are usually to be found in central-plan churches. In the central octagon at Rott-am-Inn two large altarpieces face one another against the walls parallel to the axis of the nave. Both echo the style and, to a certain extent, the proportions of the one in the choir, thus establishing a connection between them. A new form is superimposed on those revealed by a study of the plan, compromising the too perfect symmetry originally intended by Fischer. In this little Bavarian church (dating from the time of the Seven Years War), with its highly calculated intellectual design, the principles of interior architecture as laid down by Bernini have successfully recreated the triangular structure of Borromini.

Neo-Classicism

Neresheim and Wiblingen are basically Baroque churches abandoned by the creative spirit of space, and provide an arresting contrast. The high altar has reverted to its original insignificance and the Corinthian order appears. The keystones of the side arches are irremediably weighed down by urns: gone are the plaster garlands and the lively coils of scrollwork. The ends of the urns hang like plumb lines. The angels no longer fly; their attitudes are strictly realistic and their gestures resemble those of furniture removers. Here the sculptor's task is merely decorative; it is no longer his business to complete the building by attuning it in harmony with the world. Now, the decoration of a wall makes it dominant and gives it the power to shut us in. The nave at Wiblingen is on too large a scale, yet at the same time it kills any sense of expanding movement.

Technical problems

The architects of the seventeenth and eighteenth centuries cannot be credited with any decisive technical invention, which is probably one of the reasons why they have so often been misunderstood. The almost exclusive study of Romanesque and Gothic buildings has accustomed the public to associate architectural progress with constant experimentation as to systems of vaulting and the distribution of thrusts. Domes supported on pendentives and the barrel-vaulting which roof so many Baroque churches had already been perfected by previous generations.

The role of mathematics

Few other periods, however, evinced a greater interest in the concrete problems of construction. For the first time these problems were discussed outside the architects' offices and the building sites; conversely, the empirical world of stonemasonry was invaded by an alien element – science, or, to be more precise, geometry. The second thirty years of the seventeenth century were the age of the geometricians, especially in France. Like the men of the preceding century and the Florentines in the Quattrocento, they made a special study of perspective and perfected the rules to which Pozzo and his Austrian and German followers adhered in their great 'trompe l'oeil' frescoes. One of them, Girard Desargues, who was also an architect, transposed the principles of perspective to other forms of art, a fertile innovation for geometry too. Simultaneously, he emphasized that geometry's only use lay in its practical application, particularly to stereotomy; he exasperated workmen and stone-dressers set in their ways by pointing out that stonecutting could be reliably facilitated by theoretical methods and logical diagrams.

His three treatises, published between 1636 and 1640, are somewhat abstruse, but his ideas influenced both Pascal who, in about 1675, furnished Leibniz with the 'Treatise on Cones,' assuring him of its practical interest, and also Father Derand and Abraham Bosse, whose works were widely read. The great Jesuit architect, Derand, who built the church of SS Paul and Louis in Paris, gave in his 'Architecture des voûtes' a classic work on stereotomy. The work contained drawings which were the precursors of descriptive geometry and, to a large extent provided the basis for the theories of Guarini, that other architect-monk, who maintained vaûlts were the secret of his art. One plate in 'Architettura Civile' shows Guarini studying the 'Intersection of a cone and a plane,' a project to which Desargues had devoted a rough draft in 1639. Bosse, on the other hand, was writing expressly to support Desargues against both reactionary craftsmen and the Academy, and

St Nicholas in Mala Strana, Prague: section,
by Dientzenhofer (after a contemporary engraving)

his tracts were read by laymen in several languages, chiefly German. His treatise on stone-cutting was apparently standard reading in Engineering schools, as it was in the library of the school at Mézières during Monge's professorship. It seems likely that the German edition played its part in the education of the officer at Würzburg who gave Neumann his grounding in mathematics and technical theory.

The development of geometry, and the perfect-ing and enrichment of graphic representation certainly quickened the imagination of architects to bold innovations in their conceptions of space. The intersections of planes and masses sounded themes beyond the range of the Vitruvian repertory and proved that forms could be invented and played upon in limitless variations. At the same time, the rationalization of the cutting of keystones allowed these speculations to be translated into stone and resulted in difficult variations based on Roman, medieval and

Renaissance vaults. In particular, it allowed the construction of flat vaults which would have defeated the skills of the masons. Generally speaking, roofing an interior space with stone was losing its sense of adventure.

Greater precision is needed to discover whether the operation had become a mere matter of calculation, subject to the absolute rigor of mathematics. With reference to Leibniz, Siegfried Giedion speaks of 'Baroque Mathematics' and establishes a link between integral calculus and the Baroque conception of the world. The method outlined in 1684 in the 'Acta eruditorum' resembles Guarini's treatment of space, recalling the countless allusions to the infinite made by the latter a few years previously in the construction of his domes. Giedion also remarks that the three-dimensional arches at Vierzehnheiligen could have been worked out by the use of integral calculus. In this field, too, Liebniz is a dazzling example of the intellectual revolution of the late seventeenth century, giving mathematical expression, as elsewhere he did metaphysically, to all that the great church builders of Piedmont, Bohemia and Northern Bavaria were striving to translate into the medium of architecture. In the same way, mathematicians such as the Bernouilli tried to apply the new method to the calculation of vaults. It remains to be decided to what extent it moved beyond mere abstract problems or solutions on paper only, having little influence on the actual buildings of the architects who still were perfect strangers to the theory of the resistance of materials. After Neumann's death, nobody dared to build in stone the vaults which he had designed for Neresheim; they were replaced by wood and plaster versions.

Domes and vaults

The chief preoccupations of Roman, Venetian and Piedmontese Baroque architects centered on

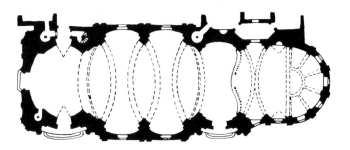

Convent Church, Brevnov, Prague: plan, by Dientzenhofer (after Koepf)

the dome. A towering dome, its drum supported on pendentives, similar in technique to those of St Peter's and the Gesù, almost invariably dominates churches in the form of Greek or Latin crosses. An original note is heard when the dome forms a direct prolongation of the walls, as at S Andrea-del-Quirinale and more particularly at S Ivo. At S Carlo-alle-Quattro-Fontane, the dome is buttressed by semi-domes separating the pendentives, and, at S Lorenzo in Turin, Guarini presents us with a 'dome' which is in fact a ribbed vault with openings; seen from outside, it resembles an octagonal drum apparently supporting the real dome. In his 'Architettura Civile' there are breathtaking examples of the wilful confusion of domes and drums, all requiring extreme technical virtuosity. From these, Vittone, the last great architect of the Italian Baroque, drew his inspiration. Domes still played a primary role in the Baroque of the Hapsburgs, until the architectural fashions of eighteenth-century Germany eliminated them in favor of saucer domes whose place lies really with the development of the vault.

Longitudinal churches and the parts of central-plan churches away from the center area were usually covered by barrel vaults. This traditional procedure, divested of any element of surprise, was given variety by the architects, who illuminated the upper sections of their naves and choirs directly from above; to do this, they had to open up windows in the vault. These being vertical, had to be connected with it, and this was achieved by means of triangular 'penetrations' or segments set at right angles to the semi-circular vault. Such a formula was capable of infinite variation according to the proportions of the segment and whether it framed the window without a transition or was linked to another small barrel vault covering a gallery. (This system was by no means unique to Italo-German Baroque; P. Moisy often refers to its occurrence in the austere Jesuit churches of France). Baroque architects found here a particularly tempting opportunity to combine two contradictory curved surfaces.

The formula led them back to a technical improvement that had been known for centuries. When the 'penetrations' grew more emphatic and increased in depth, they were almost joined to the head of the barrel vault and, finally, each bay of the nave was covered by a groined vault. The thrusts, as in some Romanesque churches and in Gothic architecture, were distributed to the angles. This resemblance was emphasized, especially in the High Baroque, by the transverse ribs and the plasterwork which traced the outline of ribs on the groins. The Theatiner-kirchen at Munich and Obermachtel are magnificent examples of the numerous churches built according to this principle, which gave rise to a double transformation, according to whether the clerestory becomes more or less emphatic.

In Southern Germany during the eighteenth century the barrel vault often became a unity, the transverse ribs disappeared, the 'penetrations' were reduced and their points were blunted so as to leave the largest possible expanse for immense frescoes. This style is evident at Osterhofen and Zwiefalten.

Further north, in Dientzenhofer's territory, the barrel vault was abolished; each bay was raised between the ribs, expanding outwards rather in the manner of an angevin Gothic vault. 'Penetrations' were no longer necessary; the corners of the vault, which resembled pendentives, formed a direct frame for the upper windows or the transverse barrel vaults of the galleries. These 'böhmische Kappen' are found not only in Bohemia, but also at Waldsassen, a beautiful church built at the close of the High Baroque era on the eastern borders of Franconia, and at Weingarten (Swabia). At Schäftlarn (Bavaria), they alternate with bays roofed by barrel vaults.

At Brevnov, in the outskirts of Prague, and at Eger, Christoph Dientzenhofer made further innovations; developing one of Guarini's ideas indicated in the design for the Providenza at Lisbon, he inserted flatter intermediary bays, lacking in emphasis, between the swelling vaults. In the ground plan, the vaults and the intervals between them are elliptical, not rectangular, in shape; the arches which bound them do not rise at right angles to the ground, but

Convent Church, Ottobeuren: plan, by Kramer and Fischer (after Koepf)

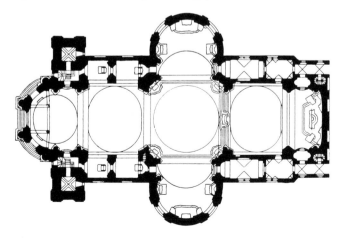

Dome of Holy Trinity Church, Salzburg, by Solari
(after a contemporary engraving)

turn inwards above the entablatures. This is the origin of the disconcerting vaulting systems at Banz and Vierzehnheiligen. In these two churches, however, the crooked arches unite at the head of the vault; each intermediary bay is reduced to two segments whose triangular shape and arrangement recall those of the 'penetrations.' In the great transept of Vierzehnheiligen, the bases of the segments do not rest on the wall but seem to be suspended between the bases of four main vaults; they are held fast by the thrusts of the vaults which find their center of balance here. In the age of integral calculus, this was the end of research into the Gothic style whose themes had haunted so many architects from Guarini onwards. It was a question of establishing a more or less closed system of interbalanced forces and of thinning out the vertical supports.

Materials

The building materials were, for the most part, those in common use during this period and indeed the previous century. Local resources remained the deciding factor; transport problems were only alleviated if rivers were close by, so that forests and quarries near the building site were always utilized first.

In any case, the architects of Baroque Europe did not usually hold stone in the same veneration as their French counterparts, and they willingly constructed their buildings according to cut-price methods, using artificial materials which were sometimes disguised by plaster. One cannot make absolute distinctions, however; L. Hautecœur recalls that Mansart had to make false walls at Versailles. Some were made of double wooden partitions filled with rubble, others of posts joined by battens. The Jesuits roofed many of the churches of the 'Assistance de France' with sham vaults. Such expedients were always a last resort, used when time or money was short. Borromini, on the other hand, apparently preferred to work with roughcast and stucco. At the Palazzo Carignano in Turin, Guarini made effective use of the ugly material, a grayish brick which does lend the undulating walls a sort of gloomy dignity.

North of the Alps, stone was often reserved for façades. This is true of Weltenburg, Weingarten and Zwiefalten where the carefully dressed tufa stone stands out oddly from the rest of the courtyard built in humbler style, of 'putzbau,' or brick camouflaged with plaster or stucco. At Rott-am-Inn, even the façade of the church is built almost entirely of this composite, since the monastery revenues were not large. However, it is significant that the wealthy abbey of Ottobeuren which spared no expense on its church used 'putzbau' almost exclusively. This did not solve other problems in building materials — the Abbot concluded that he lacked sufficient wood to fire the bricks, and was obliged to ban the export of timber from Ottobeuren territory.

Neumann's conflict with the Abbot of Langheim is also significant in this context. With the support of the Bishop of Bamberg, Neumann struggled to impose his plans for walls and vaults of stone on a master-mason who was eager enough to handle the proceeds of offerings and collections, but quite insensible to the beauty of a material which to him was linked with the foreign and outmoded. Eventually, the walls of Vierzehnheiligen were built in the beautiful golden local sandstone. Here too, Neumann, a geometrician accustomed to exact designs, had to intervene to supervize the dressing of the stone which the master of the works had neglected during the first year's work. The vaults of the church were also built of stone, in tufa, to be precise. This is relatively light, and does not seem to act in the same way as the stone of traditional vaults. It is more like a composite material, a type of reinforced concrete. After Neumann's death, his Würzburg iron supports for his vaults.

For interior decoration, the Italians used multi-colored marbles. The northern countries, on the other hand, favored wood, usually oak or lime. Many statues, confessionals, stalls, pulpits and retables were made of wood. Statues and altarpieces were often executed by artists who had come from the city. The joinery was usually done by local carpenters and woodworkers under the eye of the architect or of a painter or sculptor.

The material which typifies the Baroque, however, is stucco. The reputation of the stuccoists, like that of the large-scale fresco painters, was not restricted to one region, but extended the length and breadth of the Danube lands. Master-masons and architects summoned well-known teams, no matter how long the journey; in the seventeenth century they were mostly of Italian origin, but in the eighteenth century they learned their craft in Upper Bavaria, especially in Wessobrunn. Stucco at once replaced wood, the favorite medium of French decorators, and the marble and bronze borrowed by Bernini from classical antiquity. The material was infinitely versatile, and imposed in no way on the artists using it. It adopted a great variety of forms; the German guilds distinguished between 'Quadratoren,' 'Marmorier' and 'Polierer.' The shiny veined marble stucco often used for columns, pulpits and retables, bears no resemblance to the matt, pliant variety used in ceiling decoration, nor to the substance used by E. Q. Asam in his sculptured groups, which appears as soft as flesh and silk. In the field of statuary the technique is perfected to virtuosity. Asam spread layers of stucco over bundles of straw and pitch which were in turn set round iron rods. In this way his figures had an inner core which enabled them to make the most subtle gestures, and adopt poses that at first sight seem to defy the laws of gravity.

The organization of work

By the mid-eighteenth century, organization of work had undergone little change from preceding generations. The architect, an independent artist, was to a certain extent affiliated to the guild system, though their integration was as yet incomplete. It is significant that the German princes tried to give their architects security, were they Italian, French or German, by making them high-ranking civil servants or giving them military status: Neumann, for example, was made a colonel. The architect made the plans, discussed them with his patron, and interpreted an architectural tradition dating back to the Renaissance. Meanwhile, it was the guild masters who controlled the building sites. This state of affairs is obviously relevant to the difficulties that marked the building of Vierzehnheiligen and preceded that of Ottobeuren. On the other hand, when the master-mason was also the architect and drew up the plans himself, these problems were eliminated. J. M. Fischer and the Vorarlberg architects were fortunate in the course of their careers.

Whoever was responsible for the creation, it remained incredibly badly paid. The men who conceived the plans often received a mere token payment, a propitiatory offering which accounted for little more than one per cent of the total cost of the building. Architects had to become contractors in order to make a decent living. The Vorarlberg group, the Beers and the Thumbs were all successful businessmen. Fischer took the contract for Rott-am-Inn and Dientzenhofer did likewise at Banz. The tender only covered the labor strength; however, the client always provided tools and materials. Every spring the master-mason organized the coming season according to his resources, and the architect contractor recruited his team of stonecutters, masons and carpenters according to this. Local men were employed, and this was one justification of the vast building sites of the eighteenth century; the rebuilding of St Gallen was speeded up by popular pressure. Many specialist craftsmen brought large numbers of fellow craftsmen who had spent the winter studying at home and then crossed the Alpine passes after the thaw in the footsteps of the Landsknechte.

This was the paradox of the Baroque world, where the discoveries of the greatest scholars found their echo, and the structural forms of past ages survived unchallenged. In countries more advanced politically, socially and economically, science produced nothing more than minor technical improvements. In the ancient feudal and monastic empire occupying the center of Europe, it encouraged, directly or indirectly, the development of a new aesthetic. Among other things, one might define Baroque as the reincarnation of the Middle Ages – plus Leibniz.

Plates

Zwiefalten

151 **The Abbey Church.** General view looking towards the choir. Rococo interpretation of the Vorarlberg church is evident in the nave. The transverse ribs and 'penetrations' have vanished: Spiegler's huge fresco of 'St Benedict at the Feet of the Virgin and the Trinity' entirely covers the four bays of the nave, uniting them in a long uninterrupted expanse. In each of the side-chapels one can see a portion of the altar set at right angles to the axis of the church. Predominant color: light brown.

152 The saucer dome typical of eighteenth-century German churches. Compare with the Italianate dome over the crossing at Melk. The fresco depicts Mary, Queen of All Saints. Note the richness of the Rococo decoration, the blending of fresco and stucco, and the fine scrollwork in the pendentives.

153 The galleries on the north side of the nave. Their style is halfway between the straight built galleries at Obermachtel and the undulating lines of the ones at Banz.

154 Back of one of the stalls. The angel prolongs the movement of the scrollwork. A superb example of Rococo sculpture in wood.

155 The summit of an altarpiece.

Vierzehnheiligen

156 **Pilgrim Church.** The façade.

157 Detail of the façade.

158 The nave and choir from the organ gallery. In the center, the pilgrim altar marking the spot where Christ and the fourteen saints appeared to a shepherd in the fifteenth century. The line of nave pillars follows the curve of the gallery so as to form an oval round the altar; the main bay of the nave becomes a central space. Right and left of the benches in the foreground there is the hint of a first transept, only a small portion of which can be seen here. The central altar is dark red, and the arches of the vault old gold. Otherwise pastel shades predominate, especially in the case of the pillars and stucco work. The whole building is extremely light.

159 The choir. This is very short, containing no stalls for the monastic offices and no holy image.

160 The pilgrim altar with some of the statues of the fourteen saints. On the left, the nave gallery, on the right, the crossing of the north transept.

161 Meeting of the vaults at the crossing. Left, the great nave vault. Right, the choir vault; opposite, that of the north transept. At the top, part of the vault of the south transept. The arches resting on the four pillars of the crossing rise obliquely as at Banz, and join at the head of the vault. Note the small triangular vaults suspended between the main ones.

Würzburg

162 **The Residenz.** Section of the façade onto the gardens.

163 Façade facing the town. The traditional U-shaped plan. The main staircase occupies the left-hand section of the central block. The right wing includes Neumann's chapel.

164 General view of the garden façade.

166 The main staircase. The figure in uniform seated on the cornice is Balthazar Neumann.

167 Ceiling of the 'Kaisersaal.' Vault with 'penetrations,' frescoes by Tiepolo.

Munich

168 **The Amalienburg.** Façade. The roof of the center pavilion forms a 'belvedere' designed for pheasant-shooting.

169 Detail of the 'Spiegelsaal,' hall of mirrors.

170 'Spiegelsaal.' This circular room with silver stuccos on a pale blue background, occupies the center of the pavilion.

Pilgrim Church, Vierzehnheiligen, by Neumann
Section and ground-floor plan 1:500

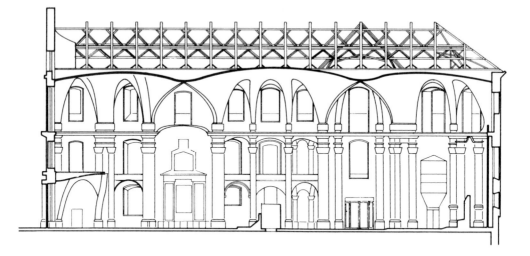

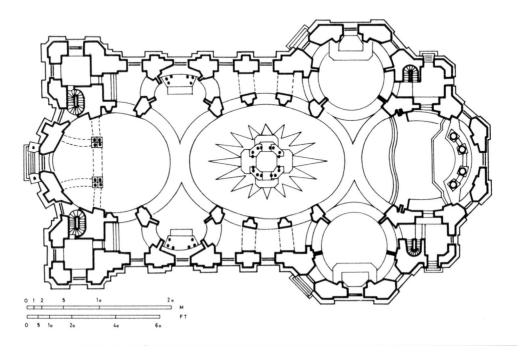

0 1 2   5   1o   2o
                                          M
                                          FT
0 5 1o   2o   4o   6o

Plan of vaults 1:300

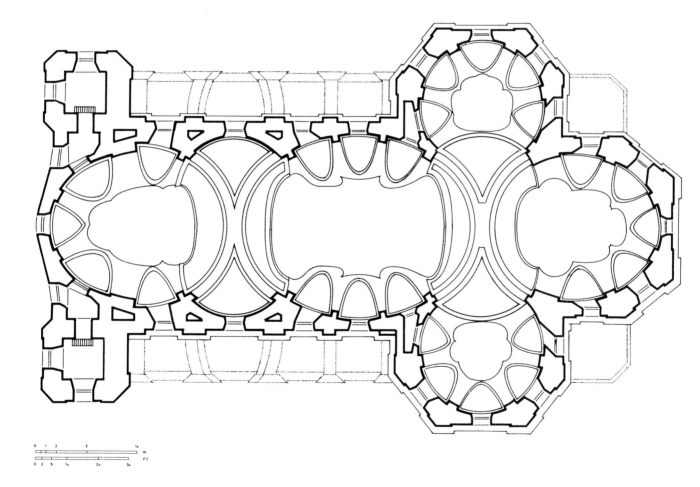

Notes

Zwiefalten

Abbey Church

Near Riedlingen and Obermachtel in Swabia. Benedictine foundation 1089-1803. Reconstruction of the church begun in 1739 by the brothers Schneider. J. M. Fischer, summoned in 1741, took due note of their plans and retained one of their towers. The great work was completed in 1747, but the decoration caused long delays of about twenty years. The dimensions are fairly imposing, especially the length: 282 feet; the width is about 71 feet and the flattened dome also 71 feet in height. Stuccos by J. M. Feichtmayr of the Wessobrunn school; statues and stalls by Josef Christian, a sculptor from the neighboring town of Riedlingen; frescoes by J. F. Spiegler.

Vierzehnheiligen

Pilgrim Church

Near Lichtenfels in the main valley, 30 kilometers north of Bamberg. Subsidiary church of the Cistercian abbey of Langheim, which paid for the building, but under the control of the Bishop of Bamberg, Friedrich Karl von Schönborn. The Bishop appointed Balthazar Neumann as his architect despite the opposition of the Abbot of Langheim who wanted to entrust the work to the Saxon architect, Krone. Work began in April 1743, following a preliminary plan, very basilican in form, drawn up by Neumann, but under Krone's direction. When Neumann inspected the work in December, he found that his rival had upset his plan by dragging the foundations of the apse too far from the scene of the vision of the fourteen saints, so that it could not coincide with the crossing as he had planned. New plans in 1744 took into account the fact that the pilgrim altar would stand in the middle of the nave. The vaults were completed in 1763, but the church was not consecrated until 1772. Statues and stuccos by J. M. Feichtmayr and J. G. Uebelherr; nave altar by J. M. Küchel. Most of the frescoes and altar-pieces date from the nineteenth and twentieth centuries.

Balthazar Neumann was born at Eger, on the borders of Bohemia and Franconia, in 1687. Apprentice foundryman in Würzburg, he learned mathematics from an officer in the episcopal army. Joined the army in 1714, and in 1717 took part in the siege of Belgrade as an engineer, then returned to Vienna with Prince Eugene. He was in Milan in 1718 and in Paris in 1723. Built the churches of Wiesentheid, Holzkirchen and Münsterschwarzach, and in 1730, Gössweinstein. In 1741 he was made Colonel in the artillery and worked on fortifications and palaces for all members of the Schönborn family, ranging from Speyer to Bamberg and Constance. His small churches at Gaibach and Etwashauser herald the vaults of Vierzehnheiligen four years later, and of Neresheim, begun in 1745. In 1748 he built the pilgrim church of Käppel above Würzburg. Neumann died in 1753.

Würzburg

The Residenz

Begun by Neumann in 1720 for Bishop Johann Philipp Franz von Schönborn, nephew of the Elector Lothar Franz. He was assisted by Maximilian von Welsch and Johann Dientzenhofer. In 1723 he submitted his plans to Boffrand and Robert de Cotte. Work was interrupted by the death of the Bishop in 1724 and did not resume until the election of his brother Friedrich Karl, five years later. Hildebrandt, who had been consulted when work was started, came to Würzburg in 1731 and 1736. The staircase and the great central rooms were built in 1742, and the chapel completed in 1743. Bishop Greiffenklau, elected in 1749, invited Tiepolo to paint the ceilings of the staircase and 'Kaisersaal' in 1753. The staircase acquired its classical decoration between 1765 and 1775.

Munich

The Amalienburg

Pavilion built in the park of Schloss Nymphenburg by François Cuvilliès for the Electress of Bavaria, between 1734 and 1739. The stuccos are by J. B. Zimmermann, the sculptures by the Verhelsts. Cuvilliès was born at Soignies in Hainault in 1695, became court-jester to the Elector Max Emmanuel, whom he followed to Munich. In 1720 he studied architecture in Paris and, in 1725, became architect to the court of Bavaria, under Effner. He worked at Brühl in 1728, and between 1730 and 1737 he produced the decorations of the 'Reiche Zimmer' in the Munich Residenz. He built the Residenztheater in 1750. He died in 1768.

The Residenz, Würzburg, by Neumann
Plan 1:1000. Elevations of façades (after Koepf)

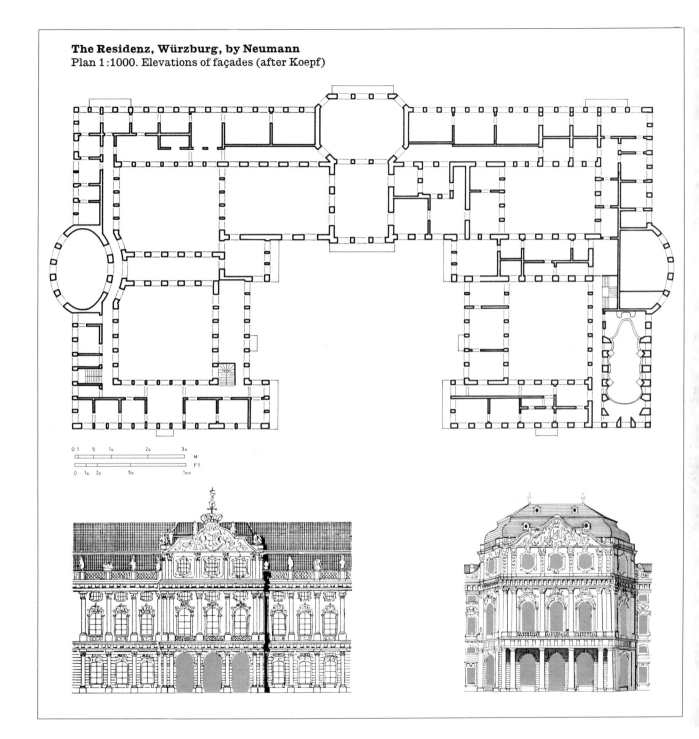

Schloss Nymphenburg Park, Munich
Overall plan 1:15,000 with the site
of the Amalienburg

The Amalienburg, Munich, by Cuvilliès
Plan 1:500

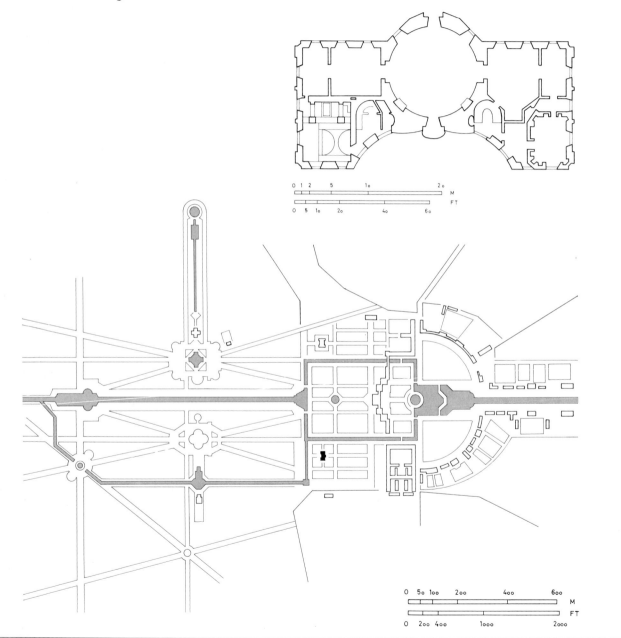

0 1 2   5   1o   2 o   M
                                              FT
0   5 1o   2o   4o   6o

0 5o 1oo   2oo   4oo   6oo   M
                                          FT
0   2oo 4oo   1ooo   2ooo

4. Secular Architecture and Town-Planning

Transformation of the Roman palazzi

The pontificate of Urban VIII at first exercised a liberating influence on secular architecture. The closed quadrilateral of the old type of Roman palazzo was turned inside out. The Pope's family had just bought the Palazzo Barberini and, when it had been rebuilt between 1628 and 1633, it was made open to the city. The arcades which had softened the appearance of the inner courts of the fifteenth and sixteenth centuries, giving the traditional 'cortile' the austere grace of a monastic cloister, now become the chief embellishment of the façade. Above them two tiers of huge windows destroy the fortress effect that we get from the wall of the Palazzo Farnese, built-some eighty years before. The plan is barely symmetrical, yet complex, representative of the new Rome. Away from the bend of the Tiber and the medieval sectors, bordering one of the rectilinear streets recently created by Sixtus V, we see a building of rustic informality containing some of the imaginative gaiety of the villas on the outskirts.

By the time the Palazzo had been completed, Bernini had been in charge of the works for four years, assisted by Borromini. It would appear, however, that Maderno, who had preceded him here as at St Peter's, had had time before his death to formulate the essentials of the building, particularly the plan with its short wings. The palaces of the next two papal families were designed by Bernini on his own, which allowed him to define some of the principal characteristics of the typical Baroque palazzo, especially with regard to the façade which now became the principal feature. Nevertheless, he did not add to the liberties taken by Maderno in the Palazzo Barberini; on the contrary, he invented new and rigid rules.

Princes and cardinals required even longer façades for their palaces, thus increasing the

173

threat of facile architectural platitudes which already menaced church façades. Not everyone could lay the foundations of an aesthetic on this requirement, as the architects of the Escorial had done; and Domenico Fontana, who executed the great designs of Sixtus V, was to experience this at the Lateran. On the other hand, there was no need to combat monotony with ornament. Bernini's first reaction was to make a strong differentiation between floor levels. The idea of the 'piano nobile' had long been established, but at the Palazzo Farnese it still does not make an obvious contrast to the second floor. Its function is neither clearly defined by its proportions nor by the accentuated line of the windows. At the Palazzo Ludovisi (1650) and the Palazzo Chigi (1164) it acquires a monopoly of pediments – triangular and segmental in solemn alternation. The upper windows have no more than lightly sketched lintels while those on the ground floor of the Palazzo Chigi are provided with embryonic over-mantels which certainly do not derive from the antique; these afford a tentative protection from the rain. This reduction of the ground floor to the level of the utilitarian and prosaic is part of a system. Its relatively rough finish gives an impression of solidity, purposely recalling the violence of the thrusts to which it is passively subject. Apart from the central doorway which is, with Bernini, still very restrained, it is no more than a pedestal. The palace itself begins above its inert mass. From now on the most prominent feature of the palazzi is the hedge of giant pilasters linking the second storey to the 'piano nobile.' Façades now stand upright; they no longer extend the length of the street, but overhang it, forming a cadence or an organism instead of a succession of layers. The pilasters do not merely break up the line of windows – grouping them like vertical iambics, a short followed by a long; they also distinguish the compact central block from the wings designed in a more relaxed style, thus creating an indissoluble unity by means of subordination and articulation.

In fact this development affected the entire relationship of the palazzi to the city; they were no longer indifferent islands against which the waves of popular life broke unnoticed, but, integrated with their individual surroundings, even dominated them. At the same time, the rhythm with which Bernini endowed his façades prevented them from being lost in the urban landscape. They no longer had anything to fear from their neighbors; it did not matter if they were modestly inserted between two bourgeois houses or between two palaces. They could not be confused with, or merely added to their surroundings, as they were no longer homogeneous quantities, but a system radiating outwards. There was no risk of the wings being submerged in neighboring buildings, as they only existed by virtue of the central block, flanking it, lending it emphasis, inseparable from it. It was left to others to transform the interiors of these palazzi. According to Siegfried Giedion, these were French architects, who under feminine influence, were careful to include every consideration of comfort in their plans. The Romans sought to make the palazzo into a constituent element of the city, a step which really belonged to town-planning.

Seventeenth-century town-planning in Rome

The history of the most famous piazzas of Rome bears witness to the precedence which town-planning held over secular architecture, and sometimes also over religious architecture. They were constructed to pre-arranged designs as was the case with the Place Royale in Paris and the Plaza Mayor at Salamanca more than a century later. The town-planners of Baroque Rome did not carve out squares, rectangles or ovals in the web of medieval alleys in order to cordon off the architecture and force it to the edge. Like contemporary church builders, they thought in terms of expansion rather than delineation. The Piazza del Popolo and the Piazza of St Peter both sprang from a central point. The expansion of these wide open spaces gradually produced an architecture in accordance with their individual rhythms. Giedion has pointed out the importance of the part played by Sixtus V who, fifty years previously, had outlined the central points of the future Baroque piazzas when he planted obelisks at the four corners of the city. For this last great patron of the sixteenth century it was a question of linking perspectives. The obelisk of the Piazza del Popolo had to close the vista of the Strada Felice, forming a counterpart to the other which brought the eye to a halt in front of the apse of S Maria Maggiore. The springtime of Baroque, however, caused this frontier post to blossom – even to become a pivotal point. Thus the twin churches of Bernini and Rainaldi – S Maria-di-Monte-Santo and S Maria-de'-Miracoli – are drawn towards the center. At the end of the following century the Piazza was linked to the Pincio by the constructions of

Piazza di Spagna, Rome: the Spanish Steps, after an engraving by Sanctis

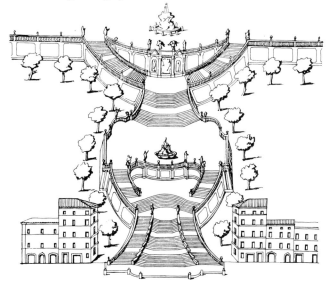

Valadier which brought order to its eastern side, thus completing its shape and defining its function in the city.

At St Peter's the development was more rapid. Twenty years after Domenico Fontana's winches had hoisted the obelisk from the Circus of Nero on to its new pedestal, the western façade of the Basilica advanced to mark out the piazza suggested by the former. The St Peter's of Bramante and Michelangelo was shut in on itself, but the seventeenth century Basilica was part of the town-plan which now began to develop. Bernini added new resonances to this relationship when he brought about the extension of the Piazza. In the case of the Piazza del Popolo, the architects took care not to break up the sense of space, and only erected buildings around it at intervals; instead of eliminating the vistas of the radiating avenue, they accorded them their full value, inserting their churches in the openings. Bernini's purpose, on the other hand, seems to be the enclosure of the Piazza of St Peter's. It is known that he envisaged a final section of the colonnade to close the oval at the east end where it is now broken. Even so, his 'enclosure' is not a real one, for, as with the Baldacchino, he has invented an ambiguous style of architecture. Far from being a wall, the colonnade is a purely spatial arrangement.

There are also numerous ill-shaped piazzas in the area contained by the bend of the Tiber, which are the involuntary legacy of former centuries. These great rents in the fabric of the city were redesigned by the architects of the Baroque who, fortunately, did not regularize them, but gave them central points. The famous fountains came into being to justify what was merely the chance enlargement of a street; they form crucial points linked to all the others by necessary connections. The beauty of the Piazza Navona undoubtedly lies in its outline – an ancient hippodrome – and it is all the more significant to note the formidable accentuation placed at its center by Bernini and Borromini to create an explosive effect. Here the creative nucleus consists of the relationship, or perhaps, conflict, between the wide façade of S Agnese and the pyramidal mass of the Fountain of the Four Rivers.

Eighteenth-century town-planning in Rome

Roman town-planners made more skilful use of architecture in the eighteenth century, taking ancient churches such as the Trinità dei Monti and S Ignazio and making them component parts of their site. As architectural creativity decreased, so town-planning came to the fore, its principles gaining diversity and flexibility.

The Spanish Steps, for example, bear witness to mastery of the third dimension. The originality of Francesco de Sanctis lies in his balance of the line of ascent with the vibrating expansion of the Seicento town-plan. At the Capitol, Michelangelo had designed a piazza preceded by a ramp; in front of the Trinità, piazza and ramp are intermingled. A contemporary drawing clarifies the structure: the staircase consists of a form of rotunda inserted between two semi-circles and the center of each of the three elements is defined by a fountain or an obelisk.

The Piazza S Ignazio, on the other hand, is dependent on the laws of the theater. In 1727 Raguzzini built three pink, concave houses like scenery, facing the gray façade of the Jesuit church. As people emerge from the obliquely set streets which separate them, they look like actors entering from the wings. The set, however, is reversible. S Ignazio can be transformed into a great back wall similar to that of an ancient theater, and we can picture the audience seated with their backs to Raguzzini's ellipses.

The stage of the Fontana Trevi does not revolve. Neither Sophocles nor Goldoni are played here, but one vast opera. The church of SS Vincenzo-ed-Anastasio seems to be there by accident. This is town-planning based on a sense of surprise and the picturesque, far removed from that of Bernini. We suddenly emerge in front of the streaming figure of Neptune, right beneath the hooves of his horses. It is no longer a question of space; it is a direct psychological shock. Perspectives were being opened up all over eighteenth-century Europe, but Rome was being transformed into a city based on sentimental emotionalism, bearing the same relation to the city of Alexander VII as the 'jardin anglais' to Versailles.

The Viennese palace

Baroque Vienna has no radiating avenues or centrifugal squares and the palaces form a random line along the ancient streets. It is impossible to see them from a distance. The streets are often too narrow and prevent one from taking in the façades as a whole, except from an angle which results in sharp distortion. Under these conditions the subtle play of proportions is bound to become somewhat theoretical and the suggestion of rhythm passes unnoticed. Particularly after 1700, the articulations are sufficiently stressed to remain recognizable at an angle of 45°, almost in profile. Fischer von Erlach and Hildebrandt in particular, transposed the themes of the Palazzo Chigi into an epic style. Stress is laid on height – the Viennese palaces usually rise to four or five storeys. The rustication at ground level is in higher relief while the lines of upper windows below the cornice lose impact. The 'piano nobile' is sometimes extended to two floors and adorned with sculpture, in addition to abstract architectural decoration. The pediments of the windows are no longer constant symbols of dignity; each horizontal series is redesigned to illustrate a particular effect. Here we have an undoubted link between the Italian tradition and

The Chancellery and garrison church, 'Am Hof,' Vienna (after a contemporary engraving)

the Northern taste for gables loaded with decoration. These exaggerated projections produce strong shadows which are stressed by the rays of the sun slanting down the narrow streets, thus giving rise to an intense rhythm.

Above all, the Austrian architects lavished decoration on their doorways. Martinelli's entrance to the Liechtenstein Palace has an inward curve and is framed by twin pairs of columns; the supporting pillars of the palace of Prince Eugene are in high relief. At the Erdödy-Fürstenberg Palace, the fine Bohemian Chancellery, and the Neupauer Palace, Atlases support balconies laden with statues. At the Kinsky Palace the pilasters taper towards their bases after the manner of Churriguerisque models and the dooorway resembles an altarpiece with secular virtues replacing angels on the volutes of the pediment. The chief result of these endeavors is the clear centralization of the façades in accordance with the Roman principle; but they also succeed in making their importance and magnificence perceptible at point-blank range. Moreover many palaces were now given two entrances of equal dignity. In some cases we come across a final result of town-planning run riot as in Prague, where Fischer von Erlach

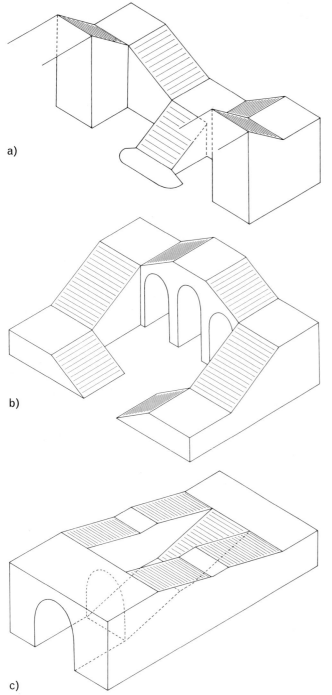

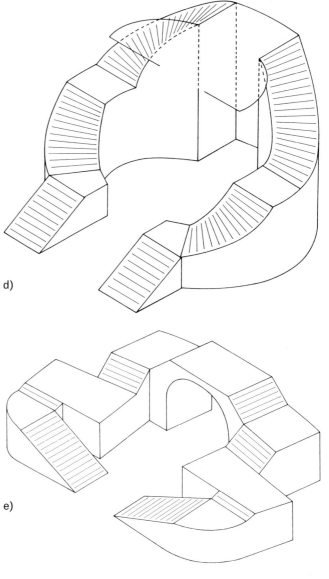

a)

b)

c)

d)

e)

Various plans for staircases:
a   Genoa University
b   Pommersfelden
c   The Residenz, Würzburg
d   Bishop's Palace, Bruchsal
e   Villa Palagonia, Bagheria, Sicily

decentralized the Clam-Gallas Palace so that one of its entrances might serve as the prolongation of an unassuming street at right angles to it.

Staircases

Beyond the doorways the heroics of tortured stone are continued in the ceremonial staircases. European architects had been developing this theme over the past two centuries and, according to Pevsner, its first variations date from Spain in the Plateresque period. The staircases at Maisons and Blois are among the masterpieces of François Mansart. In 1643 Longhena transformed the staircase of the monastery of S Giorgio Maggiore in Venice into a vast independent space. Two symmetrical flights with right-angled turns lead at first-floor level to a linking gallery whose balustrade prolongs that of the stairs. This staircase forms a unity, an individual monument, providing a changing visual spectacle as one moves from one level or position to another.

The architects of the Hapsburgs adopted the principle from men of other Italian cities, particularly Bologna, but applied it differently: their staircases do not express majestic spatial expansion so much as tension. The difference in levels must not be played down, but exaggerated; one's attention must not be distracted from the sense of weight but made almost painfully aware of it. Proportions are adjusted to meet this aim. The actual flights with their thick volutes and irregular spirals are constricted and conducive to a sense of disquiet and oppression. Compared to them, the gallery of the 'piano nobile' is as free and weightless as a mountain peak. Huge windows banish the shadows that linger at the turns of the stairs, and cherubs play round the bases of the lamps. Staircases north of the Alps are part of an actual experience.

Palaces and gardens in Vienna and Prague

The low façades of the 'Gartenpaläste' are ranged on the wide open spaces beyond the ramparts. At the Schwarzenberg and Starhemberg-Schönburg Palaces one passes straight in to the 'piano nobile,' the upper floor being insignificant. Pediments are less emphasized and the shadows less strong. Articulation is not achieved by one or more fantastically sculptured doorways, but by a rounded central position which lightens the building and softens the outline.

The development of this graceful type of architecture which, so to speak, brings town-planning into the countryside near great cities, and whose productions are as far removed from the Roman palazzo as from the traditional feudal castle, is to a certain extent linked with the glories of Versailles. At Prague, particularly in the Mala Strana, this relationship with nature takes on a different form; the gardens are actually within the city, mingled with the dignified architecture derived from the Seicento. The majority of them cling to the hills overlooking the left bank of the Vltava and, with their combinations of staircases and terraces, constitute their own style of architecture. A good example of this is the garden of the Kolovrat Palace on the slopes of the Hradschin with its tiers of loggias and open-work balustrades.

This form of stone decoration is a logical extension of the palaces of the Wallenstein district with their sharply pointed stable roofs and their loggias with pagoda-style pediments. The layout of the garden of the Vrtbov Palace is even more subtle. Stone here is no more than an armature. The main staircase is perpendicular to the slope of the hill and does not break its rhythm. Precariously balanced statues, their clothing ruffled by the wind, describe arabesques among the branches. The ramps are outlined by hollowed urns which seem to burst into flower

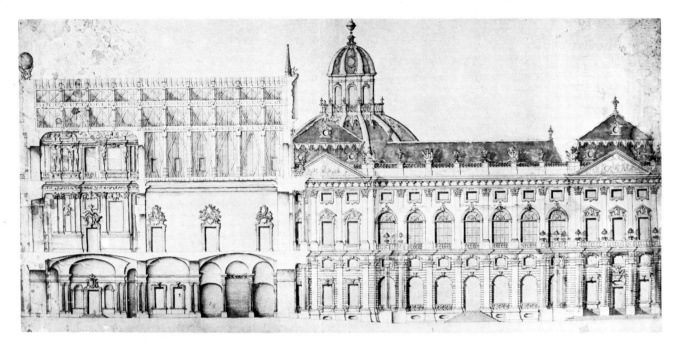

Façade and section of central part of the Residenz,
Würzburg: a typical example of the elaborate buildings of
the Baroque epoch

German palaces

The cities of Germany possess hardly any
streets of palaces similar to those in Vienna and
Prague. For when secular Baroque came to the
fore, the style of life at Versailles and Marly,
though not the outward form, had gained
inassailable prestige. This was, however, more
than a matter of fashion and taste. Several
princes, particularly those of the Church, were
on bad terms with their hereditary towns, and it
appeared that their anachronistic omnipotence
could only continue to flourish elsewhere. The
type of palace facing the open fields, isolating
and protecting the court, probably found a fresh
significance when it crossed the Rhine at the
beginning of the eighteenth century. Versailles
permitted a novel type of centralization, certainly at the time of its conception. Brühl and
Bruchsal, however, were already to some extent
the refuges of threatened feudal lords.

It was Max Emmanuel of Bavaria, ally of
Louis XIV, who began the first great program of
suburban building at Schkissheim and Nymphenberg near Munich, but the Schönborn family
were responsible for the key-works of this
particular style, particularly at Pommersfelden
near Bamberg, and Würzburg.

From the point of view of function and
situation, Pommersfelden is no more than a
provincial château. It was not built to serve as

180

the principal residence of a sovereign and his court, though it has the dimensions and grand style of a palace. Pommersfelden is a genuine product of a condemned system: the first building payments were provided from the bounty paid to the Elector Lothar Franz by the Emperor Charles VI after his succession to the throne. It is also a genuine product of Baroque imagination: the part played by the architect Dientzenhofer and professional craftsmen was relatively small; it was Lother von Schönborn who conjured up the palace, with its tremendous staircase and useless rooms, in the lordly fashion of one who builds entirely for his own pleasure. The staircase only gives access to the first floor but its galleried well fills the entire height of the central pavilion; beyond it yawn the empty spaces of the marble drawing room with its giant pillars. Below, a low, cool hall in rustic style, with walls of shells, recalls 'nature,' and at the end of an enfilade, a tiny

Schloss Nymphenburg: overall view
(after a contemporary engraving)

'hall of mirrors' with a marquetry floor is filled with the countless reflections of Chinese porcelain. Needless to say, Dientzenhofer and his craftsmen were not the first to invent such creations, but for the next fifty years or more they formed a standard pattern for architects of competence or genius to make lyrical poems of the palaces of Germany. At the Bishop's Palace in Würzburg the building program is better defined but the actual operation was slower and more tentative. There was a clear recourse to architects in Paris and Vienna, though these were not decisive. Both Robert de Cotte and Boffrand provided plans, the latter visiting the Schönborn in 1724; Hildebrandt came to Würzburg in 1731. It was Neumann, however, who had the last word. He was wholly responsible for the chapel and was commissioned to build the staircase and the 'Kaisersaal,' thus setting the seal of the Schönborn on the palace. Despite its classical balustrade the staircase is more Austrian in style than its counterpart at Pommersfelden. At Pommersfelden it was Lothar Franz's pleasure to place the two staircases in a much too vast space; the two tiers of loggias and the 'trompe l'oeil' paintings at the base of the ceiling arch contrast with the staircase, giving the visitor an immediate feeling of height. At Würzburg there is again a conquest of the third dimension, but without the nervous tension of Fischer von Erlach and Hildebrandt. On the first staircase landing Neumann releases us: we turn and find that the staircase expands in two parallel flights above which is the upper gallery, its balustrade lit from the windows behind; over all hangs Tiepolo's frescoed ceiling.

The small châteaux of Germany

The plans for the Würzburg staircase were drawn up by Neumann about 1735. In 1731, at Bruchsal, he had designed to a circular plan the most dramatic of his staircases for another member of the Schönborn family, the Prince-Bishop of Speyer. In 1744 Clemens August von

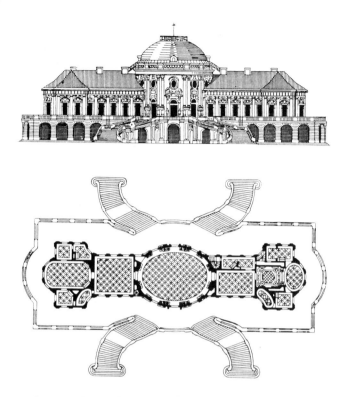

Château Solitude, Stuttgart: façade and plan,
by La Guépière (after Koepf)

Wittelsbach, Archbishop of Cologne, summoned
him to Brühl where his local architects had been
unable to furnish the Schloss with a staircase
worthy of it.

Simultaneously with the deployment of these
indispensable imperial themes in their vast
official palaces, the German Princes discovered a
taste for smaller, more intimate, châteaux. The
undoubted reason for this lay in the great
success of many French architects, some of
whom were victims of the Revocation of the
Edict of Nantes.

Each principality had one in its employ. In
Saxony there was Zacharie Longuelune, in
Prussia, Jean de Bodt, and in the Palatinate,
Nicolas de Pigage, who completed Schwetzingen

and built the 'Gartenpalast' of Benrath in the
Elector's Westphalian domain. In Württemberg,
La Guépière was appointed chief architect in
1752 and was responsible for Solitude and Mon
Repos. To a certain extent, these two palaces
near Stuttgart, like Benrath, reproduced the
standard design of Hildebrandt: two low wings
framing a rotunda. The powerful Baroque
articulations of the façades are, however, more
or less dispensed with. Friezes with triglyphs, an
unyielding line of balustrades at roof level and
right-angled pediments over a series of four
coupled columns indicate the influence of
French classicism while the domed central
blocks resemble Vaux-le-Vicomte rather than
the precincts of Vienna.

A few years earlier the Belgian architect,
Cuvilliès, who had been trained in Paris during
the Regency, had played a similar part at the
court of Munich. His masterpiece, the Amalienburg, a simple hunting pavilion in the park at
Nymphenberg is still smaller than Solitude, or
Benrath. It consists of a circular salon, surmounted not by a dome but by a terrace used for
pheasant shooting, and four modest rooms. The
decoration of the interior walls, however, is
indicative of the victory won by the Rococo over
Germany between 1734 and 1739. Here, as elsewhere, it slyly monopolizes space, but its
abstract patterns have lost the Jansenist stiff-
ness so often to be found in the churches of the
period. Fragments of scrollwork are intermingled with palms, branches of walnut-trees
and trophies of war and hunting. Coils of silvery
stucco deprive the wavy cornices of any independent form and overflow onto the ceilings:
they are fashioned into fountain jets, tritons'
tails, and wonderful shrubs blending the contradictory elements of dead twigs and bunches of
leaves ruffled by the wind. Simultaneously the
Rococo invaded the salon of the Princesse de
Soubise in Paris, and the 'Reiche Zimmer' in the
Residenz at Munich.

German Baroque in relation to the countryside

In seventeenth-century Germany exterior design and the discovery of harmony between architecture and its setting were phenomena relating to the country rather than the town. Town-planning as such only succeeded in the execution of abstract building schemes of cosmopolitan origin, as at Mannheim. Outside the cities architects tried one formula after the other: palaces were protected by parks in the manner of Versailles. There were the formal flower beds of Schleissheim and the Lake of Mon Repos, a harbinger of the Romantic period. Nevertheless, it was religious architecture which managed most successfully to harmonize with the countryside.

One of the most famous pictures in Central Europe is probably that of the Abbey of Melk, whose buildings crown a spur overhanging the Danube, offering to the entire valley a dignified church façade framed and ennobled by two pilastered pavilions. A few miles downstream the tower of Dürnstein rises at a bend of the river.

Göttweig Convent: overall view (after a contemporary engraving)

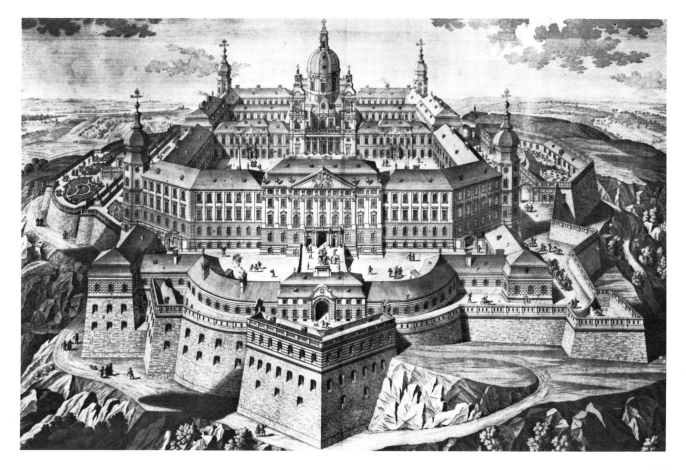

Chronological Table

Date	Historical Landmarks		Date	Central European Baroque
1618	Defenestration of Prague			
1620	Defeat of Czechs at the Battle of the White Mountain			
1623	Pope Urban VIII			
			1628	Completion of Salzburg Cathedral; start of Jesuit building at Innsbruck
1643	Battle of Rocroi; death of Louis XIII			
1644	Pope Innocent X			
1648	Peace of Westphalia			
1655	Pope Alexander VII			
			1656	Birth of Fischer von Erlach and C. Moosbrugger
1659	Peace of the Pyrenees			
			1660	Birth of Franz Beer and Prandtauer
			1661	Solothurn Jesuits; Kempten Abbey
			1663	Theatines in Munich
			1668	Passau Cathedral; birth of Hildebrandt
			1669	Prague: Czernin Palace
1678	Treaty of Nijmegen; birth of Vivaldi			
			1679	Prague: Church of the Knights Templar
			1681	Birth of Peter Thumb
1683	Defeat of Turks at Kahlenberg		1684	Lobkowitz and Liechtenstein Palaces at Vienna
1685	Revocation of the Edict of Nantes; birth of Bach, Handel, Scarlatti		1685	Birth of D. Zimmermann; Waldsassen and Käppele churches
			1686	Obermachtal; birth of C. D. Asam
			1687	Birth of Neumann
1688	Fall of the House of Stuart			
			1692	Birth of S. M. Fischer and E. Q. Asam
			1694	Salzburg: Holy Trinity and University Churches
			1695	Town Palace of Prince Eugene
			1698	Birth of Cuvilliès
1699	Peace of Carlovtsi (Turks lose Hungary)		1699	'Gartenpalast,' Schwarzenburg; Smirice Church; Berlin Palace
1700	Spanish War of Succession		1700	Belvedere ('Gartenpalast' of Prince Eugene)
			1701	Fulda
			1702	St Nicholas in Mala Strana; work begins at Melk
1703	Peter the Great founds St Petersburg			
			1710	Brevnov (Prague); Banz

Date	Italian Baroque
1624	Birth of Guarini
1625	Bernini begins the Baldacchino
1629	Genoa University
1630	The Salute, Venice
1635	SS Luca-e-Martina
1638	Interior of S Carlo-alle-Quattro-Fontane
1642	S Ivo
1643	Staircase of S Giorgio Maggiore
1652	S Agnese
1656	Throne of St Peter's; S Maria-della-Pace
1657	Colonnade of St Peter's
1658	S Andrea-del-Quirinale
1662	Assumption, Ariccia; Guarini in Paris; Ste Anne-la-Royale
1663	Palazzo di Propaganda Fide; S Maria-in-Campitelli
1664	Palazzo Chigi; façade of S Carlo-alle-Quattro-Fontane
1665	Bernini in Paris
1667	Death of Borromini; Capella di SS Sindone, Turin
1668	S Lorenzo, Turin
1669	Death of Pietro da Cortona
1680	Death of Bernini
1683	Death of Guarini
1691	Death of Rainaldi

Date	Historical Landmarks	Date	Central European Baroque
1711	Emperor Charles VI	1711	Zwinger Palace, Dresden; Kiritein
1714	Peace of Utrecht; Leibniz' 'Monadologie'	1714	Vienna: Karlskirche and Kinsky Palace
1715	Death of Louis XIV	1715	Schleissheim; work recommenced at Nymphenburg; Wiengarten
		1716	Weltenburg
		1717	Rohr; Pommersfelden Château
1718	Peace of Passarowitz (Prince Eugene conquers Serbia)		
		1719	Saar: St John Nepomuk
		1720	Würzburg and Bruchsal begun; Einsiedeln
		1722	Frauenkirche, Dresden
		1726	Osterhofen
		1728	Steinhausen
1729	Canonization of St John Nepomuk		
		1730	Prague: St John Nepomuk, 'Reiche Zimmer' in the Residenz, Munich; châteaux of Bruhl and Poppelsdorf
		1732	Diessen; Schäftlarn
		1733	St John Nepomuk, Munich
		1734	The Amalienburg
1740	Accession of Frederick II and Maria Theresa; Austrian War of Succession	1740	Zwiefalten
		1743	Vierzehnheiligen
1745	Madame de Pompadour	1745	Meresheim; death of Hildebrandt
		1746	Wies; Birnau
1748	Treaty of Aix-la-Chapelle	1748	Ottobeuren
		1750	Death of E. Q. Asam
		1753	Death of Neumann
		1755	St Gallen; château of Benrath
		1758	Rott-am-Inn
1763	End of Seven Years' War	1763	Altomünster; La Solitude
		1766	Death of Peter Thumb, D. Zimmermann, and J. M. Fischer
		1768	Death of Cuvilliès
1772	First Partition of Poland	1772	Wiblingen
1773	Suppression of the Jesuits	1773	Buchau
1780	Death of Maria Theresa		
		1783	Rot-an-der-Rot

Date	Italian Baroque
1715	Venice: Church of the Jesuits; Villa Palagonia, Palermo
1723	The Spanish Steps, Rome
1729	Juvarra: Stupinigi hunting lodge, Turin
1732	S Maria-della-Morte; Trevi Fountain
1733	Façade of S Giovanni-in-Laterano
1737	Basilica of Superga
1738	Vittone: Valinotto Chapel
1742	S Chiara-di-Brà
1770	Death of Vittone

Farther still, the vast bulk of the fortress-monastery of Göttweig would have dominated the entire plain above Vienna if Hildebrandt's plans had been realized. The great monasteries of Germany, on the other hand, do not all enjoy such classic pictorial settings; but most of those which underwent lavish reconstruction in the eighteenth century, form original harmonies with the landscape in which they are situated. Their relation with the soil is purely functional and unconnected with any form of aesthetic. From this viewpoint Baroque abbeys share some features of contemporary communities.

In the case of the pilgrim churches there seems to have been a systematic search for the picturesque, though the abbots and the Baroque artists did not pick the sites. Whether the sanctuary overlooks a lake as at Birnau or a town as at Käppel, the perspective is worked out and the relations between the three dimensions carefully studied. At Vierzehnheiligen, Neumann abandoned the traditional east-west orientation, turning the church so that the axis linking the high altar and the central altar could be prolonged across the Main as far as the monastery of Banz. His aim was not merely to guide and encourage the pilgrims, but to give a plan to a section of the valley, erecting an idealized form of postern near the spot where the river entered Schönborn territory. Other architects assumed less dominating relations with the landscape, concealing their churches for as long as possible in order suddenly to reveal them at the turn of a path or the end of a wood. Wies is an example of this type. It lies in front of a back-cloth of mountains whose curved outlines blend with its roof.

These are famous examples; but there were countless pilgrim churches which transformed hills little known outside their own district. Parish churches, too, decorated the fields of Bavaria with their bulbous towers; abbeys founded small priories in remote villages. Thus Baroque sculpture was scattered to suit the needs of popular worship. The role played by St John Nepomuk throughout Central Europe is well known: his sculptured silhouette, surplice flying in the wind, crossed by the oblique line of a crucifix, can be found affectionately perched on the parapets of village bridges recalling the bridge at Prague from which he was flung to his death, and which about 1710 the sculptor Brokoff transformed into the most beautiful Baroque bridge in the world. This prosaic form of decoration with its reminders of Bernini is of overwhelming significance. Here, the forms and rhythms of the second Roman Renaissance rediscover their ancient affinity with water, this time far removed from the fêtes, the parks with their echoes of mythology, and the fountains with their learned imagery. Supposing we had to choose a type of exterior space from the Baroque lands north of the Alps corresponding to the piazzas of Italy, we should perhaps find it at Holzkirchen, a tiny village in the diocese of Würzburg. At its edge a stream stocked with ducks and geese flows between an octagonal chapel by Neumann and a statue of St John Nepomuk. The intellectual and emotional sides of Baroque combine to transfigure this haphazard collection of farm and ecclesiastical building. Having permeated a whole area of Europe, speculations on the central plan and studies in emotive sculpture unite beside a highway in Franconia.

Bibliography

General Works

Les Architectes Célèbres
General Editor: P. Francastel. Paris, Mazenod, 1959.
(Articles on Bernini, Borromini, Longhena, the Churrigueras, Fischer von Erlach, Cuvilliès)

Giedion, S.
Space, Time and Architecture. Cambridge (Mass.), Harvard University Press, 1959. (See Part 2)

Mâle, E.
L'art religieux de la fin du XVIe, XVIIe, et du XVIIIe siècle. Paris, A. Collin, 1952. (Iconography)

Pevsner, N.
An Outline of European Architecture. Penguin Books, 1943, 1954, 1957

Tapié, V. L.
Baroque et Classicisme. Paris, Plon, 1957. (Present and past civilizations)

Wölfflin, H.
Principles of Art History. London, 1932

Monographs

Argan, G. C.
L'architettura barocca in Italia. Milan, 1957

Argan, G. C.
Borromini. Milan, Mondadori, 1952

Bourke, J.
Baroque Churches of Central Europe. London, Faber & Faber, 1958

Brinckmann, A. E.
Von Guarini bis Balthazar Neumann. Berlin, 1932

Brinckmann, A. E.
Theatrum Novum Pedemontii. Dusseldorf, 1931

Colombier, P. Du
L'architecture française en Allemagne au XVIIIe siècle. Paris, P.U.F., 1956

Fiske Kimball
Le style Louis XV, Origine et évolution du rococo. Paris, 1949

Franz, G.
Bauten und Baumeister der Barockzeit in Böhmen. Leipzig, V. E. B. Verlag, 1962

Grimschitz, B.
Wiener Barockpaläste. Vienna, 1947

Gurlitt, C.
Geschichte des Barockstiles in Italien. Stuttgart, 1887

Hauttmann, M.
Geschichte der kirchlichen Baukunst in Bayern, Schwaben und Franken. Munich, Schmidt, 1921

Lieb, N.
Barockkirchen zwischen Donau und Alpen. Munich, 1953

Lieb, N. and Dieth, F.
Die Vorarlberger Barockbaumeister. Munich-Zurich, Schnell & Steiner, 1960

Pinder, W.
Deutscher Barock. Königstein, 1957. (Die blauen Bücher)

Powell, N.
From Baroque to Rococo. London, Faber & Faber, 1959

Portoghesi
Guarini. Milan, Electa, 1951 and 1956

Venturi Perotti, M.
Borromini. Milan, Electa, 1951. (Coll. Astra Arengarium)

Wittkower, R.
Art and Architecture in Italy, 1600-1750. Penguin Books, 1958

There are numerous other monographs, notably: 'J. B. Fischer von Erlach,' by H. Sedlmayr (1956); 'Balthazar Neumann, Leben und Werk,' by M. H. von Freeden (Berlin-Munich, Deutscher Kunstverlag, 1953); 'Die Brüder Asam,' by E. Hanfstaengl (Berlin-Munich, Deutscher Kunstverlag, 1955).

For individual German churches readers should also refer to the 'Langewiesche Bücherei' (Königstein im Taunus) and, above all, to the 'Kleine Führer' (Schnell & Steiner, Munich-Zurich).

Acknowledgements

The Editor of the series extends his thanks to the Library of Art and Archaeology at Geneva who kindly provided hitherto unpublished drawings of Italian Baroque plans, once part of the Fatio Collection and reproduced in this book on pages 11, 12, 15, 95, 139 and 140. Thanks are also extended to the Department of Engravings of the Museum of Art and History at Geneva for the reproduction of Fischer von Erlach's plans on pages 53 and 54.

Professor Hans Koepf of Vienna graciously allowed the reproduction of the series of Baroque plans on pages 52, 58-61, 64, 100-102, 105-107, 130, 142, 143, 171 and 182, which are taken from 'Deutsche Baukunst von der Römerzeit bis zur Gegenwart,' Deutsche Bauzeitung, Stuttgart.

The reproductions in the Preface, pages 6, 7 and 8, come from Reinhard Friedrich, Berlin.

Finally, for unavoidable reasons, the photographer was forced to use three existing photographs, for which he thanks the owners. They are of St Nicholas in Mala Strana, page 67 (Photo Plicka, Prague); St John Nepomuk, page 70 (Photo Paul, Prague); the Abbey of St Gallen, page 82 (Photo Gross, St Gallen).

Table of Contents

List of Plans and Maps accompanying text

List of Illustrations

Jacket: interior of the dome of S Lorenzo, Turin